Learning to Love:
On the Way of Experience

Learning to Love:

On the Way of Experience

BARBARA WRIGHT GEORGE

Epigraph Books
Rhinebeck, New York

Learning to Love: On the Way of Experience © 2019 by Barbara Wright George

All rights reserved. No part of this book may be used or reproduced in any manner without written permission except in critical articles or reviews. Contact the publisher for information.

Paperback ISBN 978-1-948796-59-0
Hardcover ISBN 978-1-948796-64-4
eBook ISBN 978-1-948796-65-1

Library of Congress Control Number 2019936049

Book design by Colin Rolfe

Epigraph Books
22 East Market Street, Suite 304
Rhinebeck, New York 12572
(845) 876-4861
epigraphps.com

This book is dedicated to my mother, Carrie Cross Brady, and to my friend, Pauline de Dampierre. Two intelligent women.

Also, this book is dedicated to Claudia and Kristine, and of course, to Jim.

By his example and guidance, Lord John Pentland gave me and many others a treasure of great price.

The cover art is a detail of one of my own paintings. It was made after seeing a similar Persian miniature at the Metropolitan Museum in New York City, in the spring of 1984. Several years later, my mother sent me the transcript of a PBS series. She had marked the following passage:

> *On the tree there are two birds, fast friends.*
> *One eats the fruit of the tree, and the other, not eating, watches.*
> **–Joseph Campbell, quoting from the** *Rig Veda*

When the idea of learning how to love first came to me, I remembered my painting and the quotation my mother had marked. These birds, sketched 30 years ago, seemed to represent a direction for living, and they continue to inform me.

Real love is the basis of all, the foundation, the Source.
  –G.I. Gurdjieff

Contents

Preface	XI
Beginnings	1
The Dark	9
The Cold	13
The Heat	18
Black Pepper	25
Jazz	29
Music	32
Sitting Quietly	39
Early Mornings	44
Solitude	48
Being Loved	52
My Parents	56
My Neighbor	62
My Companion	66
My Enemy	70
What Is Difficult	75
What Is Easy	81
Not Knowing	85
Not Too Busy	92
Disappointment	96

Truth 102
Order 105
The Idea of Death 108
Myself 117
Life 119
Acknowledgments 122

"And the observable world
Longs to flourish in your love."
–Rainer Maria Rilke, "Turning-Point,"
Translated by Stephen Mitchell (*Material for Thought #9*)

Preface

Everyone knows, or at least suspects, that a person who is loved will thrive. Some people know that a plant or an animal or any living thing that is loved will flourish and grow strong. Not everyone knows that a person who is *able* to love will be transformed—I had to find that out for myself, and I did—by learning how to love.

It's easy to love someone or something one's attracted to, and it's easy to love when life goes well. But I wanted more. I wanted to know how to love—and be able to do it. This meant loving *all* the people in my life and *all* the parts or aspects of my life, as often as possible in all kinds of life conditions. A very large goal, but why not? Perhaps I wouldn't live long enough to come close to the final goal, but I could begin, and in beginning, I found that almost no condition is so difficult as to prevent learning. In fact, the people and aspects that comprise my life want to be "learned."

Remembering my own experiences of the energy of love and wishing for the joy those experiences gave me, an old-fashioned word comes to mind. I remember feeling joy *bestowed*—a gift. Yet it was clear that something was up to me. I needed to learn *how* to love, and I needed to begin by giving my attention to some unacknowledged and unloved parts of my life, which in spite of everything wanted to drag me down. How to do this was not as clear as knowing what was needed, but I found my way. As my study deepened, so did the meaning of love. I realized that it appeared on a scale, ranging from complete freedom and completely harmonious presence to a new feeling of simply liking something or someone, but always, at whatever level, with some measure of heightened awareness, joy, and energy. I also realized that having loved something or someone even once, directly, without expectations or requirements, free of thoughts or overlaid images, I could never again *not love* that thing or that person. I could forget to love, but in remembering, love in all its joy and energy returned. This love had no opposite—it was either there or not there. And more and more often, I could find it again and it was there.

Along the way, I began to keep notes. Writing the notes became an important part of my experiments and more and more helpful, first when writing them down—especially when I tried to record directly while new observations were coming to me—and later, when thoughtful reading brought new insights and I added new notes.

This book is a collection of those notes made over a period of several years in my journal, date books, and random notebooks, on concert programs and various loose slips of paper. Living a busy life, I wrote them down in a variety of locations in Canada, California, Colorado, and Pennsylvania, and in a variety of places, including hotel rooms, airplanes, trains, and several different train or airport terminals. Notes like these, of dreams, thoughts, memories, and new experiences, are mostly interesting only to the person who keeps them, or later on, perhaps to family members or close friends, but as my notes began to coalesce around the aim of learning how to love, I came to believe that some parts of them might be of interest and a help to a wider readership. I hoped that something might be evoked in anyone reading them—not so much an evocation of previous knowledge, but a call to the forgotten ways of being and loving we all share. These records tell what happened as a result of my experiments. They also describe a method that can be followed.

Although I kept brief notes in the beginning, the puzzle of how to be able to love—from *myself*, by my own choice rather than being pulled into place and compelled to like this or dislike that—kept me gathering more and more material. The study both deepened and widened. I realized there were not only areas of my life which I definitely did not love, there were some I tried to avoid, some I hadn't even noticed, and some that had once been loved and now lingered, neglected. These were the areas I wanted to learn to love, perhaps for the first time, or once again.

Many of the avoided, unloved or unappreciated areas of my life were physical—the hot, humid heat of the East Coast or the brisk, cold temperatures of the Rocky Mountains were a challenge to an older body. Sometimes I noticed a kind of pride in my unique stance against something—not for me toe-tapping jazz or the black pepper in almost every dish prepared and served in restaurants. There were other things that I wanted to like more, such as order and solitude, early mornings and getting more rest. I wanted to understand what it might mean to be able to love my neighbor or my enemy, and how to love several things even *more*, especially my parents but also music, and truth. The necessity began to grow in me to face the idea of death, which at this time of my life more than ever needs to be faced. Necessity prompted me to explore disappointment, a negativity that still has the power to destroy—although its power has been weakened by seeing more clearly what this feeling means. It was also necessary, essential even, to understand and explore the dark, heavy atmosphere of my new home in Toronto, which is why—and where—my aim to learn how to love began to come to light.

One question has haunted me for many years. How to live actively in the world I see around me and at the same time attempt to live in another world, a transcendent world comprised of the finer energies experienced in quiet inner work? After several years of these experiments, some words came to me as I sat quietly on my cushion one early morning, on a wintery day in Colorado:

You can meditate, learn mindfulness—but it's best to learn to love everything. Every single thing I see is a tiny bit of this world that is being created—and destroyed—at every moment. When I am able to see it, it's vibrant with life.

That winter morning, I realized once again that learning to love was the Way for me. Years of dedication to inner work had helped to reconcile the lack of harmony I saw in my outer life, but it hadn't always benefitted the people in my life, or the details of my own life. The search for presence had led to moments of new awareness and new experiences of consciousness—but only some of the time. So the words given to me that winter morning were a precious gift. They asked me to see more—to see all of life. I knew that for me this meant loving all of life. These words helped me feel that this direction toward seeing and toward love, which I had chosen, was mine—my own—and therefore right for me.

It was winter outside when I heard those words, but the sun was shining into the room as it rose above the horizon, lighting up the colors of the rug where my cushion was placed, reflecting light off the wood floor, penetrating my closed eyelids. I felt just then, in that moment, I did not want to be in any other place. I was in my own place, and truly that place, inside my body and in that room where I sat, was vibrant with life.

Wishing to be able to see all of life and to love it, what did I try? How did I experiment? Right away it became a study, an investigation. I tried to see as clearly as possible just what a person or an object or a particular quality truly *is*, with as few associations, thoughts or images as possible to obscure the truth. The practice of self-observation in the Gurdjieff work has some of the same characteristics. Self-observation begins by including, or *remembering*, the whole person who is there observing at that moment and then observing directly, without analysis. The practice of self-observation is difficult, but at moments it can result in real feeling for oneself and for what is seen. And further, in itself, this practice is an instrument of change.

During these years of study, I sometimes created a new experience by intentionally setting up a situation in order to see it directly—something as simple as experiencing darkness by repeatedly sitting in a dark room, exploring a large quantity of black pepper as a new taste on my breakfast eggs, or leaving a window slightly open on a very cold night. However, for some aspects of my life I could only sit down and ponder, staying right there in front of something as large and unexplainable as the idea of death, trying to write as I sat there facing it, or at other times, taking a new look at an old experience, such as a long-held belief in my unlovable nature.

As the months passed, there were some successes, which gave me a new impetus and supplied new energy to go on. I had help from the past in the form of still living memories, such as memories of loving the cold as a child, which reappeared to help me love sleeping in a cold room as an adult. Dreams also helped. Sometimes a dream from the night before was just what was needed to help me understand an experience the next day. For example, early on I had a long dream about three couples who were having many troubles in their marriages, but by the end of the dream each couple had come together and reaffirmed their love. The dream concluded with a kind of pronouncement, which my own experience has proved true: *The most precious thing is the ability simply to see another person without being taken by how they manifest.*

Do I love all the parts of my life now? Yes and no. There were some areas that were in fact almost too difficult, such as loving jazz, playing the violin every day or getting more rest. I haven't given up completely, but there may not be many possibilities there. However, I am still learning. And there are still areas of my life yet to be explored.

I want this learning to continue the rest of my life because a change has taken place in me as a result of this study and these experiments. Learning to love one area of my life seems to strengthen my ability to learn in another area, and results accumulate, mysteriously, invisibly, and undeniably. More and more often, I find myself surprised to be different in outer life, to be closer to the ideal I wish for. More and more often, I find myself surprised by delight—in the fact of life itself, and especially by seeing the beauty of human beings as they struggle to live. Feeling the relaxation of my body, feelings, and mind more often makes me happy and more wisely available to the world and to other people. I have learned some important things. I have learned how to see more deeply, how to study, and how to love. It is my sincere hope that if this has been possible for me, anyone can do it. But it is more than a hope. I know it is true.

> *"One word*
> *Frees us of all the weight and pain of life:*
> *That word is love."*
>
> –Sophocles, *Oedipus at Colonus*

Beginnings

Many books and articles have been written and many talks and classes have been offered about love—and the need for love. Teachers and religious leaders urge us to be more loving, to find love, gratitude, and forgiveness, to be compassionate. And rightly so. It's easy to see the absence of love and the results of this in our world—the despair, poverty, violence, and more—that flourish in the absence of love. It's not as easy to see this in our own lives, and to accept that it's true, but we feel it. We know that something is missing when love is not there.

Like most people, my life has been touched from time to time by love—and by its absence. My life has been full of bright intelligent people and beautiful places. Yes, I've lived with the absence of love, and sorrow and resignation often filled that empty space. But it is easier and less painful to remember the good of my life, and there was much good.

For many years, motivated by the question "Who am I?" and inspired by Gurdjieff, I have tried to see my life clearly and observe myself in it—to understand more deeply my purpose in this particular life and get to know some of my own quirks, talents, drives, and motives. Over the years, I have also had glimpses of something that could be called *higher* behind the manifestations of this person I call myself, who lives the day-to-day life. There is something else, more central to my being, which might be called a higher nature, and also there is something even higher, which may be the source of life. It's all a gift, and I have been given much. Thanks to my teachers, a practice, and grace itself, I have received many rich experiences and have tasted the divine on more than one occasion.

My life has required keeping just the right relation between the inner and the outer currents, with their little ripples and eddies—the various parts of a person that make us who we are. In outer life, I was a history teacher, a musician, an artist, and most recently, an editor and a Feldenkrais practitioner. When necessary, I supported myself and my daughters financially. At the same time, my inner life was supported by a daily inner practice, assisted by studying Gurdjieff's ideas and working with others in groups and in the study of crafts. I've tried to help other people find their own purpose. It was not always easy to balance the demands of daily life and a feeling of urgency coming from some unknown center of my being that wished to understand my place in the universe and the purpose of my life. Maintaining a right relation was challenging, but in spite of the ups and downs, including the big world-wide shocks since the first years of the new century, and some big shocks in my own life during this time, events in both the inner and outer currents continued to flow. Then my outer life changed. After forty-five years in San Francisco, I entered into a new marriage and life in Canada and found myself living in a new city in a new country.

The first years of that new life were wonderful years. Many self-imposed demands for perfection relaxed, and with a commitment to marriage and the stability that came with it, some of the fears that plagued my adult life disappeared. I felt my heart opening to other people, whether that person was my new husband or someone I met in the street or in a shop—this new relaxation allowed my heart to open more easily. There was much to explore in this new city, with interesting places to visit and interesting people to meet. And, I slept better, which was also new. More often than not, I'd wake up in the morning with the luxurious feeling of having slept well. Being in love and being loved seemed to create happiness. One night in particular during those early years still lives in my memory.

After a day of good meals and good talks, and a long walk on a path in a nearby ravine, I fell asleep that night thinking, *I am completely happy.* Earlier, when I was younger, there hadn't been many days of happiness like this, such memorable happiness. Now, late in life and newly married, there it was, and I welcomed the awareness of being alive that came with it. Quietly, without much effort I relaxed into sleep, sustained by the thoughts, feelings, and sensations of being there, happy and *alive.*

I remember this because a special dream came to me that night and, writing now, the images and the *taste,* and some of the meaning of that dream, are all still vivid. It was one of those dreams that shine with color and life, and like a play or a movie, have a fully realized locale with living characters playing their parts. It was one of those dreams that had meaning and knowledge that would fill pages, although it probably lasted only a few minutes.

In the dream, I was in a small town and the people who lived there were moving around in their usual ways all over the town. I was standing on the grass in the front yard of a house in the town, and I was happy. I was completely happy, filled with an energy that was very light, the color of gold, translucent, and so vibrant with movement that I could barely contain it. Immediately, I knew that this energy was the source of my happiness. There seemed to be no difference between this pure, lively energy and what I knew was happiness. At the same time, I knew in a way I didn't understand, that this energy was *love*.

Then, I became aware that I was holding a little boy in my arms. He was small, maybe two or three years old. He wasn't crying but I could feel his profound sadness, and the reason for his unhappiness was obvious. He had no legs at all, only a perfect little body that ended at the base of his pelvis. In the way of dreams, I knew very clearly that when he wasn't lying in bed, someone had always carried him, but he wanted to move by himself. He knew what it would be to have legs and run or walk, and play as other children played. I could feel an enormous longing in him—a longing to be the same as others and able to move. Feeling his longing, my heart ached and filled with my own longing to help him. Almost immediately this took the form of a wish. I held him closer, feeling the pain and confusion in his little body, and wishing with all my heart that I could help.

He began to relax toward me, and feeling his relaxation, I knew what to do. There was a way he could learn to move on his own. He needed to find this by himself, so I would give him time alone on the grass or on a blanket inside where he could explore and figure out how to be upright. I knew he could do it. He would need to learn how to balance on the base of his body—that legless pelvis. Then, he could learn to move, just as some babies born with legs move along the floor on their bottoms. He would need to learn balance and confidence first, but it was possible. Wordlessly, I assured him that it would be all right, that this would work. I would help him help himself, and he would learn. While I told him this, my arms held him closer. I felt my whole body embracing him, sheltering him, loving him. The energy I had felt that was happiness—or love—filled us and surrounded us.

Before in special dreams, a voice had told me the meaning of the dream. Now this same voice spoke again, telling me, *"This is the energy that Christ used to heal people."*

Immediately, I knew this to be true. This energy of love that was all around us, filling my body completely, making it vibrate with feeling and the sensation of being alive—of course, this was healing energy—the energy of Christ—sacred energy. I knew at that moment this little child would be healed.

With this knowledge, my mind and heart were filled with even more love, and with many more new thoughts and feelings. Surely the dream lasted only a few minutes, yet in that short time, everything I'd studied and heard about Christianity, the religion of love, took on new meaning. And what of Gurdjieff, I wondered? He called his work *esoteric Christianity*. Immediately, those two words illuminated an understanding of both Christianity and Gurdjieff's teaching, an understanding that deepened and expanded, wordlessly. Alongside this new understanding, there was a vivid glimpse of energies—all the energies in the cosmos, level upon level of energy—from very slow, coarse, even sluggish energies to those that were very fine and vital, and finally to an energy so fine and so alive that it seemed to contain everything. Everything.

I opened my eyes and lay in the dark next to my sleeping husband, pondering what I had just been given. *Love is an energy.* I couldn't understand well enough why that was so important; perhaps this meant that what I had taken for love before was simply its quality or its effect, the way it made me feel, what might be called the contents of love. And, remembering my dream and its message that love is the healing energy, I was certain of my need for this energy in order to heal others and myself. But I also understood that I needed to *be able* to love.

Of course, remembering one's needs doesn't last long without renewal. The demands of my new life didn't help. Living in Toronto continued to be interesting. My life became more and more busy. We traveled frequently to cities in Canada and the United States, visited France, Costa Rica, and Romania, and went to Philadelphia once a month. I continued my regular visits to Colorado. But between trips, I missed my life in San Francisco. Increasingly, I felt too busy; and my family and friends on the West Coast seemed too far away.

Several years passed, and the life I had committed to in this marriage began to feel more like an exile, less filled with energy and life, and more and more difficult. The oppressive darkness of the long Toronto winters, the heavy heat in the summer, the constant demands, and the long distances from my family and friends weighed me down. All this became almost overpowering. My doctor had a name for it, Immigrant Depression Syndrome, also known as Ulysses Syndrome, a mythic name for extreme homesickness. Being from Ireland, she told me how she'd gone through it herself. Missing my family and friends, my light-filled apartment, the weather and year-round gardening in California, missing the exchanges with others working along the same lines, missing most of all the weekly meetings with people my age—yes, Immigrant Depression.

Believing that by now, at this age, I should be able to live through even big changes without feeling stressed made it worse. I thought my anxiety was under control many years ago, that now I could be reasonable and calm under any circumstances. But this was no longer true. I was forced to see myself as powerless, completely in exile. And along with the feeling of exile there was a diminishing of my feeling for living. There was less enjoyment, more and more dread of dark days and dark rooms and the too-loud energy of the main street that passed in front of our building, more and more unwillingness to be open and direct with others—and worst of all, almost without my noticing, my deep love for my husband was also diminishing. There were moments of relief that kept me moving—but life became very difficult. I could understand William Styron and other sufferers describing depression as something dark and heavy. It felt just like the short, dark days and dark rooms of a Toronto winter, where people dressed in black seemed to fill the streets, their faces slightly strained, braced for the weather to come.

Finally, and fortunately, the approach of another winter with its promise of gloom jolted me awake to my situation. I needed to be active, and looking around inside for how to do this, I found this thought—*I need to learn to love the dark.*

How to do that? I started my experiments in learning to love both figuratively and literally in the dark. In not knowing, and in the dark itself.

To learn to love the dark, I sat in the dark—in a chair, at a table, on the couch—trying to experience what *dark* is and what I feel in the dark. Does darkness itself depress me or do I have associations of darkness that do this? Does it frighten me or help me relax? I found it necessary not only to try to see the dark as such but at the same time, as much as possible, to know myself and what this seeing was evoking in me. As I continued, unexpectedly my body began to relax. I felt less tension, and at the same time, the darkness itself seemed to change. It became warmer, so to say, and not the *cold*, heavy emptiness I had felt in the condo during earlier winters. Happily, a few tentative memories emerged so I could relive a few old memories of sitting in a totally dark room and being relaxed and at home in myself, which added warmth to my new experiences. This was the beginning of loving the dark. Some characteristics of love gradually appeared, such as relaxation and quiet joy. There even were evenings when I waited before turning on the lights, simply to enjoy being there.

That new relation to the dark was my first experience of learning to love one part of my life, and yes, Reader, I learned to love my husband again, in the same way—by simply trying to see him more clearly, and at the same time, trying to see myself while allowing the simple impression of him to enter my heart and mind. This love might not have had the same intensity as that of the first years of marriage, but as it deepened, I valued it more and more. Most precious of all, though, was the fact that I began to love *him*. Not who he was or had been in the world, what he'd done or said for others and for me, not his good looks. I simply began to love *him*. There is no other way to describe it. This influenced many other aspects of my life and taught me how to go further in learning to love.

Over the last few years, I have learned several things about love. Now, I know it is possible to love intentionally, from myself, not because I should or just because I'm attracted. And, I've learned not to be greedy because love manifests on many levels, from moments of simple, relaxed appreciation to pure, unifying joy. Even a single particle of the energy of love can change the world, and this energy in any of its forms can heal and create happiness, in me and in the world around me.

Yes, I still get tired and discouraged. Dark feelings still emerge, but I try to stay with them, just as I stayed with the dark, to feel them and understand them *as such,* to come closer to loving them. In their darkness, they remind me that transformation occurs under the light of awareness fueled by the energy of love. It's true what Sophocles wrote—love frees us from the weight and pain of life.

The Dark

How to face the cold dark days of winter in Toronto? I noticed that I am not the only one who feels the strain of winter—the faces of people in the elevator, people in shops, or on the subway say more than words—no one seems to like the winter weather here, with its short dark days. Almost everyone has something negative to say about it, yet almost everyone, native and newcomer alike, simply shrugs and copes with it, making jokes, and pretending it's not so important.

But I wanted something different. I have put on good attitudes before and found ways of accepting situations—thankfully, I found ways out of some—while creating the semblance of normalcy. But for me, a change of attitude wasn't enough. It didn't go deep enough. It wasn't always reliable. In order to live happily in Toronto, I needed to be able to love deeply, loving the people who live here and the place where I live. And especially, I needed to be able to *know* the dark, maybe even to love it.

How to do that? This wasn't the first time I began something from a place of not knowing. That's what beginning is about for me, almost always. And, not knowing anything means everything needs to be learned. But how to begin? It came to me to learn more about the dark by experiencing it closely, so as to know what it is.

Darkness comes early in the day in Toronto, moving into an already dimly lit north-facing apartment, filling it right up to the corners. On the first evening as I began my experiment, it was after 7 o'clock and the living room was dark except for the light coming from the kitchen and Jim's desk lamp in his office. Outlines of chairs and plants on the deck were dimly lit by the ambient light from the office buildings in the distance. Turning out the lights in the kitchen, I sat quietly on the living room couch and noticed the lights outside this room—the desk light and the ever-present glow of the city lights. Right away, I observed something interesting: I don't see the dark. My eyes always go first to the light.

After that first evening, whenever it was possible, I tried to sit a little longer in the living room without turning on the lights and to keep my vision enclosed within the dark in the living room as much as possible. This began to evoke a subtle feeling, a beginning feeling *of* the dark—not so much *about* the dark or how it makes me feel, but of the dark itself. I began to feel or sense the quality of darkness. I began to be aware of this quality. Music has a similar quality, which is unique and almost indescribable in words. Music can be heard by more than the ears; it can be heard by the whole body, especially what is behind the notes. As I begin to feel the dark, I realized that because it has no form, no notes, harmonies or melodies, it can be *listened to* more directly than music. It soon became very clear that like listening to music, this kind of listening requires practice.

Soon, when out in the world, I began to notice that the edges of things are dark—the risers of the escalator steps, the trim around the wall panels down the hall. Dark, and also a shadow that outlines and emphasizes objects, a shadow that has color, such as Payne's grey, reds, and blues. I remembered discovering the color of those shadows in my watercolor days. Yet, dark itself—does it have a color? I began to question this. Perhaps it can only be known by its action as it has no taste, scent, sound, or color. Is its action only to obscure, just as light's action illuminates? Is dark merely the absence of light? I was left with the question of what in fact dark *is*.

And my own reactions? *Why does the dark make me sad? Is that an action that comes from the dark itself or from the absence of light? Does something in me associate darkness with sadness? Why does sunlight, even a bright lamp, make me feel brighter?* Not being able to sort out what is action and what is reaction, I returned to how this experiment began.

I wanted to be able to love the dark, especially the dark that cuts the length of the day so quickly now in late afternoon. I understood more deeply that I needed to know it better, and as I sat more often and longer without a light, with only dim light from outside, the dark felt thick, but not heavy. It enveloped me but was not unfriendly. My body began to relax, to feel a tentative happiness in living within the dark's silence, if only for a moment or two.

A new discovery: there's silence in darkness. The silence I have experienced when I work quietly at sitting is charged and vibrant with life. Is it the same for darkness, I wondered. My wish to understand and through understanding to love, became deeper. I wrote several paragraphs while in a dark room, sitting within a small area of light. Then I turned off the last lamp that allowed me to see the paper and my fingers holding the pen, and for a moment everything was allowed. Everything was still.

In the silence, my body relaxed even more, and a clear memory from another time came back to me. It was from one of my first years in college. It happened a long time ago, yet it returned again, full of life. I remembered myself there, the young intellectual, smoking cigarettes and reading late at night, downstairs in the newly finished room in my parents' basement. At last I finished a chapter, closed my book, lighted a final cigarette, and turned out the lights. Immediately, the room was completely, totally dark. In this solid, thick darkness the only light was at the end of the lighted cigarette. So many years later, it's still difficult to put into words the feeling of that moment—the feeling of a question. *Do I exist?* Only the red spark of the cigarette was visible, clearly alive, and yet at the same moment, I knew I was there holding it. How do I know I'm here, I wondered. Stubbing out the cigarette, I sat there in a room with no light at all, a room filled completely with darkness, aware. A thought came to me: *I cannot see my body or anything else yet I know I am here.*

A few minutes went by—or maybe an hour. I sat there in the dark experiencing a feeling of myself that was new, yet in no way unfamiliar. It was as if all the trimmings of who I was—who I thought I was—fell away in the silent depth of darkness.

Writing these words, which are difficult to find, there is a beginning understanding of darkness. Perhaps, the action of the dark is to reveal what is inner and hidden—it allowed me once to know a hidden, secret presence that resides inside all the trimmings and trappings of who I think I am. And now, when I remember to feel its quality, the dark gives me a new kind of relaxation that is not simply the absence of tension; it is the feeling of a new energy, which is steady, more available, more reliable. This energy acts as a reminder of my presence. It tells me I am here. And it gives me the ability to listen more quietly and to hear more truly what is "behind the notes" when I am with other people, facing difficulties, or my own weaknesses. It helps me in beginning to love the dark.

The Cold

Winter, Colorado

Waking up in Lafayette, Colorado at 2:00 a.m. to close the window, I am torn between wanting more fresh outside air and the fact that it's simply too cold. When we drove back late last night from Boulder, the temperature had fallen to 4°F; now it's 14°F. Outside the window it's very dark and very quiet. The darkness and the silence create an atmosphere hardly touched by the light from a lamppost across the way or from the stars.

It happens a lot these days—I learn something from my body. My nose is in love with the cold. It loves the uncomplicated feeling of very cold air. The moment of impact when the air hits the face and comes into the nostrils is always new, and in its newness, delicious. At the same time, breathing this cold air feels familiar, as if I've known it before— from childhood, from young womanhood, perhaps from another life in some long ago cave or high country meadow. The familiarity of it rouses memories of all kinds of experiences and all kinds of feelings— feelings of freedom, choice, strength, presence, of simply being there, and other feelings not so easily named.

I remember many moments of being out in the cold air, and these memories call up vivid pictures. I see myself walking to school as a child all bundled up in thick wool pants over tan cotton stockings held up by suspenders worn under my dress. My mittens are attached to a knitted cord strung through one coat sleeve, inside the coat across the back and out through the other coat sleeve so they can never be lost. On my head there is a brown knit hat. It has decorative flaps halfway up the sides that frame the face and resemble wings, and long thick ties that can be fastened under the chin or hang loose to stand in for the braids Hans Brinker's sister wore.

When I was in third or fourth grade, the book *Hans Brinker, or The Silver Skates* made a big impression on me and, when it was cold enough in our high-altitude but sheltered valley, I happily pretended to be Hans or his sister Gretel, trying to skim along on the ice patches on the sidewalks while thinking about him and his family and their hand-carved wooden skates. So much of the book was about self-sacrifice, trying to put the other person first, and in the end, about redemption. Walking to school along icy sidewalks, I often thought about Hans and Gretel and their friends skating on the canals and wondered what it was that Hans felt so deeply that he let a friend—who needed it more—win the precious prize, the Silver Skates? How could he do that after practicing and working so hard? Could I be that good, ever? My own feelings for my friends, my family, and especially for my sisters were seldom like his, and seemed terribly selfish. And now? Am I still as selfish as I was then? I still wonder about this, and think about it sometimes when I'm on a walk, even though I'd almost forgotten Hans and Gretel until the cold reminded me.

Sometimes on my walks I try not to think, allowing all the sights, sounds, and scents around me to come in. Sometimes I try to think, intentionally; choosing something that needs to be looked at and then letting other thoughts drift in and around it so they can be seen more clearly. For me, walking now or as a young woman is the same as walking when I was a child. It's a time to think—at least that's how I call it—although others might call it daydreaming. It was, and is, essential to me. Becoming a grownup hasn't changed that. However, while remaining much the same, my questions about things have changed shape and in many ways have become simpler. Questions about such things as self-sacrifice and why I couldn't be more loving also seemed to have grown up, and in growing up, to require a much more all-round view, and a steadier pace that comes with getting older.

More memories come back to me now of walking to school and home for lunch, walking back to school after lunch and then home to play or read or listen to the radio until it was time for supper. There's another vivid image of a later time. I am in my mid-twenties, walking to college classes at 7,703 feet above sea level under a brilliant blue sky. The sun bounces its light off snow almost too white and too bright to look at. In January, the average low temperature here is −8°F but this year's January is even colder at −32°F and each day it never gets warmer than 0°F. It was a good place to seriously begin learning to love the cold. As I walk to class, the moisture inside my nose begins to freeze but it's not too far to the campus and I will arrive in time to keep the outside of my nose from freezing, too. My body moves easily. I am wearing leather Indian moccasins with good soles, sides high enough to tie around the ankles, and only one pair of socks, but my toes don't complain about the cold as they did when I was a little girl. My old car built in 1928 hasn't started for days but it doesn't matter. The three of us—my two young daughters and I—always walk. One walks to her first grade classroom and escorts the other to nursery school, and I walk to the college classrooms where there is a delightful variety of history courses and opportunities to play the violin. On good days, in good weather, the car is only used for grocery shopping, visiting friends in the country, collecting wood for the cook stove, or driving down the mountain for the two and a half hour trip to Grand Junction and my parent's house. The big, warm house... my dear parents... my lovely daughters...

Happy to remember, and to be where I am and who I am just now, letting the memories float around in me, I go back to sleep.

I am awakened at 7:00 a.m. by a golden square of light on the far bedroom wall. It's the sunrise, red and gold on the horizon. Almost every bit of me was under the covers, leaving just enough space to breathe—my head is wrapped except for mouth and nose with a little room for my eyes. In fact, remembering how animals curl their paws over their noses, I've propped an edge of sheet a couple of inches away from my face, so the air breathed in is warmed just a little by my own breath.

Waking to the sunrise and remembering where I am, there is a new feeling of certainty in me about both the past and the present. I know without any doubt that I was fueled then in those young years, as I am now, by a kind of joy. Joy in discovery. Joy just to be alive. Later on, in those cold college days, some of the joy came from reading sacred ideas, by a hope of consciousness that opened my heart and mind and gave warmth to my body. The blessed joy of being alive and knowing that such ideas were also alive—that is what warmed me then, and it still does.

Throwing back the covers, I lie there. The room is very cold, although it's warmer than it is outside, and I'm glad I closed the window. It's cold but I am not afraid of it. The feeling of freedom helps me. There is a faint memory of a new obedience, a new taste of a wish appears, to find and know for myself the meaning of *Thy will not mine*. It's not only knowing what I want to do today—or what I should do—but wanting to find again the experience of *I wish*.

Getting up and moving into the day, I discover again the other side of the cold: warm well-being. A hot shower, a wool sweater, the thermostat set to go on at 7:30 a.m., warm feet from the vent under the basin in the bathroom, a cup of hot tea and a fire in the fireplace. Does the cold help me to feel the warmth more deeply? I have experienced both cold and warmth this morning. In truth, underneath their outward manifestations and the particular way they touch me, each is unique and a simple experience of what it is, one enriching the other and adorning the experience of life with unforgettable moments.

The Heat

SUMMER, PENNSYLVANIA

First the dark and then the cold—from learning to love these qualities, I remembered some important impressions and learned some new things about myself. Learning to love the heat seemed like a logical next step. And what better place to begin than Pennsylvania with its hot summer temperatures reinforced by high humidity. We've been here several weeks at a time for more than a few summers. This summer seems especially hot.

Now, as I write, there is a more and more demanding work with heat. In order to truly experience the heat, I must first, at the least, be able to tolerate it. Not yet, however.

At this moment, it is raining outside, steadily, and it is cooler, much cooler than yesterday, although it's still very warm in our room. Each time we've come here in the summer the heat has been a challenge. We have been here three days and each day has been very hot. Whether one is moving or not moving, it's all the same. The heat overwhelms me. Remembering when we here for a week last summer, when the heat and humidity almost overpowered me, I wondered how it would be this year, and after a few days, I know. It's already difficult—uncomfortable to move, sit in a chair, or sleep. What to do? I could simply give up and stay in an air-conditioned room but that would be surrendering, admitting that learning to live with the heat—and to accept it for what it is—might be impossible.

How to find an attitude that would be helpful and give me a chance to learn to like the heat and lessen my body's reactions. There seems to be something that I don't want to acknowledge, a fact that might just be true—my body is in charge. I've caught glimpses of this fact before, seeing the subtle influence the state of the body has on the thought and the feelings, and I've decided that the mind cannot tell the body how to be any more than one can tell the ocean not to rise and fall with the tides. I also know that when all my parts are united toward a single goal or a single inner event, such as creating art or love at its best, the body takes its place, cooperating with the whole person—mind, heart, and body. Then it's a willing, important part of the wholeness of myself, which can honestly contribute to the art and act of living.

Remembering the very hot weather when I was young, there is little or no memory of being overwhelmed by the heat, and I wonder what has changed. The air was very dry, but it was very hot, often in the 100s. Yet, as a child I loved to play outside. Once another girl and I tested the idea that tea was cooling—I'd read that somewhere—so we sat out on her porch sipping freshly brewed hot tea. It was not cooling. We dripped sweat but drank it all anyway. No complaints.

All the children in my neighborhood played outside all day even in the hottest days of summer. Sometimes we walked across town to the swimming pool or downtown to a movie on Saturday morning. No one drove us in a car. And, I seldom wore shoes even though my grandmother had scolded my mother early on for allowing me to be so *unladylike,* going outdoors *barefooted.* I even learned to walk on hot sidewalks, carefully—and very quickly—with a few experiments of trying to put my mind elsewhere *fakir* style while willing my feet not to burn.

Not always successfully then; impossible now. Of course, my body is very different now, older, wider, taller, with different attitudes—more *trained* by life.

There was a time last evening when a little shift of attention appeared in me, when my too warm body was just *that*, when a separation took place. For a moment there were two: myself and my body, but it happened too quickly to allow any relation that could be called or felt as respect or love. Now, I am distracted by discomfort. Rather than looking directly at this sweaty body, I decide to think about how to love.

I begin to recognize and appreciate that love is too often hidden behind the trimmings we take for love, such as family obligations or the thrill of physical attraction. What do I really know? I know that the first step toward love is awareness, and that awareness begins with separation, that is, with each part being seen simply as itself, not merged by the ordinary thought into an indistinct unity. I know that real unity begins with real separation, which requires an awareness that is very clear, simple, and direct.

Unfortunately for us human beings, this awareness is not always present in us; we have forgotten it. Fortunately, it can be cultivated. Awareness can be re-learned and used, up to the point where grace—a kind of higher awareness—begins. Taking the first step toward love—really trying to be aware, to *see* the object I wish to love—allows clarity to appear. This new clarity can enable the parts to be themselves, functioning as they were meant to function, and real unity can result. The person who is loved and the person who loves are two individuals, yet within the clarity of this separation, they are parts of one harmonious event. They are one.

Enough of thought. A little later I notice the rain has stopped. It was a steady, soaking rain. The earth was completely receptive, not quite the happy receptivity I felt in Colorado where the dry, brittle heat had become so dangerous. Here there was a kind of joy, but a mature joy more appropriate for the East Coast—more grownup, more sedate. Only the almost instant, greening response of the grass and weeds quietly betrays its happiness.

And the heat after the rain? My body is alternating between a fairly normal physical state and one that *exudes* moisture. My hair is wet, my face is slippery and wet, the back of my shirt is wet. Not damp. Wet. In fact, I seem to perspire more when sitting very quietly, relaxed and not moving. The heat seems to arise from inside my body, and along with the heat outside . . . it is very warm. It is also very humid.

Along with greening the grass, the rain has left even more moisture in the air, even more than earlier in the day. Will I ever be able to value this heat? Probably not. Feeling defeated, I decide that to be able to simply accept it would at least be a beginning. Perhaps then I could learn to tolerate the heat. But liking it or loving it? That seems too far away, too precise, too fragile a feeling to stand up against my physical discomfort, which I can see no reason to embrace. Feeling defeated, I surrender.

Summer, Colorado

We left the overhead fan on last night, set at the next-lowest speed. Earlier in the evening we visited a friend whose living room ceiling fan created a lovely coolness without air conditioning, but sleeping more or less directly beneath the fast but silent revolutions, my body was too cool. About 2:30 a.m. I got up and turned the fan off. Once again I had a question about this body I live in. Can my body adjust and be more flexible in the way it receives the outside world? Must it always be slightly in revolt if conditions are not perfect?

During the ride to the Toronto airport a month ago, I wondered about this and asked the driver, who obviously was from India, what he thought about living with heat. He said that growing up in India, his family never used air conditioning, but in Toronto his passengers expected the car to be air conditioned, so he himself had gotten used to it. Surely there was a time in human history, I thought, when we didn't expect so much and our bodies were more adaptable to hot or cold weather or with living alongside too many people or only too few or food that was either plentiful or scarce. I thought about cold-blooded animals and their adaptation to the temperature they lived in. I thought about bears hibernating. Finally, I thought about Laurens van der Post's stories of the Kalahari Bushmen and the physical and attitudinal adjustments they made *willingly* to their environment.

The memory of how it feels to come out of an air-conditioned building into the heat reinforces my curiosity now. The body seems to feel much hotter after it's been air-conditioned. I remember my first visit to Toronto. It was summer and the first time I went down to the street from my husband's eleventh-floor, artificially cooled apartment and stepped outside into the hot humid air, I could barely stand up. My head was dizzy. I felt faint. It took several minutes before I could walk down Bloor Street to explore the downtown shops as I'd planned.

All these thoughts returned and bothered my sleep last night, and after I turned off the fan I was determined to find a way to relax and sleep. By then, the air was cooler so I was able to relax and sleep until I was awakened a little before 7:00 by a subtle shift of the weather outside. My body had registered the very moment when the sun reached a certain point in the sky and the day's heat began. Noticing this gave me a glimpse into the vast, intricate inner world of the human body and its mechanisms, a world governed by sensation.

Reminded by the unique taste of inner sensations, I remembered walking a trail thirty years earlier at Mesa Verde in New Mexico, trying to understand the people who used to live there. In order to experience the daily life of the people who lived so long ago in clusters of rooms built against and within the cliffs—those mysterious people, unknown today in spite of the large, complex buildings and the utensils they left behind—I walked a dirt trail from a *kiva* up a small incline to the parking area, trying to be fully alert to everything around and outside my body.

Listening, smelling, seeing. Trying to be aware of everything "out there." With no room for thoughts or feelings or interior assessments of the exterior world, I felt alive and aware only of the world around me: the heat, the texture of the dirt and small stones on the path under my feet, the scent of the sage brush, which looked dry and only slightly lighter in color than the path, but thick enough to conceal animals or human enemies. My listening became more and more acute, seeming to emanate from my whole body—front, back, sides, bottom of feet, top of head—all listening and fully alert.

Unexpectedly, there was no fear, no images of wild animals or native warriors. I had become a living body moving up a path in the hot, dry air that danced all around me and was filled with life, seen and unseen. I had become part of the landscape, as if my body served a double function. Through sensation and movement it protected itself while at the same time allowing me to see, hear, and feel what was around me. Without any thought at all, I loved being there, knowing this sacred land.

This morning, I recognized the same *sensitive* sensation in my body I experienced in Mesa Verde. It awakened me just at the very moment when the cool of the night air became the first note of daytime heat.

Another Summer, Colorado

This morning I was awakened by the smell of smoke. A huge wildfire in the mountains was making its presence known even here fifty miles to the south. This was a morning for closing windows and turning on the air conditioner—for protecting the body. I remembered my experience on that Mesa Verde trail and wondered if I could find the same kind of *knowing* I had found on that Mesa Verde trail. I wished for the sensation of that as I sat quietly this morning, finding and losing the silence, losing and finding it again. It came to me as I sat that love always begins with awareness, which makes knowing possible. And sometimes, when there is enough of it, knowing is very much like being, and very much like loving. Perhaps at their highest, finest manifestation, they are the same. It seemed so on that trail thirty years ago.

Another Summer, Pennsylvania

This is my tenth summer here. It is hot and humid. My hair is constantly wet. My body is uncomfortable. But something has changed. Something in my attitude has relaxed. I wouldn't want to live in the East Coast summer heat permanently, but it might be possible. Something has changed. Most likely it's a kind of adaptation, a change of attitude, as well. But there is a taste of something new, a separation that lasts longer now—I am present and aware of body, mind, and feeling. There is a hint that with all these parts helping each other—and helping me—I might learn more than tolerance of the heat. I might someday learn to love it. At least it's a beginning.

Black Pepper

After my first experiments in learning to love the dark, the cold, and the heat, it became more and more evident that the field of study was enlarging. There was a lot to discover and to observe. So much was unknown to me—little things, such as my food choices that excluded several quite healthy selections or my dish washing preferences that too often excluded someone helping me, and big things, such as the way I dealt with disappointment or the fear of death. At the same time, it was clear that all of this, large and small, known and unknown, was part of *me*, of who I am in this world. And all of it needed to be seen and included, accepted and loved, if at all possible.

A few summers ago, I had a struggle, which was not quite successful, an experiment in learning to love the humid East Coast heat. At the same time, being already in struggle mode, it seemed as good a time as any to begin eating—and loving—something different for me. Black pepper.

For years, I had refused anything with black pepper in it. It burned whatever it touched: lips, mouth, and throat. And it upset my stomach for hours after eating food flavored with it. Maybe it was an allergy. Maybe it was simply not liking the burning sensation. Maybe it was an educated dislike. Whatever the reason, I refused.

Growing up in a medium-size Colorado town in a middle-class family, I was not aware of ethnic cuisines. The food we ate at home or in restaurants was seldom extremely spicy or too peppery hot. My mother's chili was delicious, full of flavor, but never too *hot*, and so good that I wish I still had her recipe. But tastes have changed. After moving to San Francisco, I was introduced to more exotic menus and learned to like many new tastes and flavors—except the dishes with lots of pepper, red or black.

More and more often now, pepper seems to be an ingredient that no cook can omit, and therefore, I've been increasingly wary in restaurants or when visiting friends who pride themselves on their up-to-date cuisine. There have been too many times when I forgot to say "No black pepper" and wasn't able to eat what was served.

I still remember such an event in a very expensive restaurant in Boulder, Colorado, which was famous for their specially prepared hamburgers. Being somewhat a collector of Best Hamburger Memories, and still savoring the memory of a Zim's burger in 1970 San Francisco, I dearly wanted to try the Boulderado's burger. But it was not meant to be. The meat was pre-seasoned with black pepper before it was even cooked, and therefore, for me, ruined. I don't remember what I ate instead of the hamburger, but the disappointment still lives in memory.

After years of disappointment and subservience to my body and its likes and dislikes, I finally reached my limit. I wanted to be free, and wanting that helped my wish to learn how to love. The time had come to learn to love black pepper.

Why do I forget that doing something intentionally changes any situation radically? I know it's true, for example, that fasting intentionally is not as painful as being deprived of food by someone else. The same thing is true of sleep. Intention adds a new element to any situation. What is intention? Where does it come from in me? What I call intentional doesn't always have the power of adding something new, and may not be as intentional as I believe it to be—some little thought or feeling may have passed through my mind, and I have called it the beginning of an intentional act, which has very little staying power. But I know, and must remember, that when I am present, and act from that *presence,* intention has power.

That summer we were in the country near Philadelphia with twenty-five other people for a very warm summer week of intensive inner and outer work. Many demands were made on one's ability to remain present. This did not include fasting, however. Normal meals were served. In fact, the meals were better than normal. The kitchen team went out of their way to prepare and serve only the best foods—fresh vegetables and fruit, organic meats, very fresh eggs, delicious cheeses and dairy products, most of it straight from neighboring farms or farmers markets. It was during this week, with this food, that I began the black pepper experiment.

The first time I asked my breakfast partner on the left to pass the pepper, he registered a moment of surprise and without comment handed me the pepper shaker. Calmly and deliberately, I sprinkled those previously disliked black flakes on my egg. Calmly and deliberately, I took a portion onto my fork. Calmly and deliberately, I placed the portion in my mouth, chewed, tasted, swallowed. And, it wasn't too bad. The power of intention!

Each day of that week, while struggling with the heat, I continued to use pepper on my eggs at breakfast. Sometimes I put a great quantity, as I've seen others do; sometimes I was more artistic. Each day the combined flavors of salt, egg, and pepper began to feel more *comfortable,* and by the end of the week a new element had taken its place in my breakfasts. I had learned to love the taste of black pepper.

Like most moments of first love, that week created strong impressions, in particular, of early mornings in the old stone barn, breakfasts with many friends, and eggs with pepper. And now, whether the egg is soft-boiled, fried, or scrambled, the sight of small black specks on top of the lovely yellow of the egg-yolk no longer offends me. Almost every morning now, some years later, I have a little breakfast practice. Salt the cooked egg first, then a light dusting of turmeric, followed by black pepper. It's a lovely sight and one whose taste continues to delight me.

Is it really love? One morning recently during another visit to the country place near Philadelphia, several of the cooks overheard me saying "I love black pepper!" and challenged me. I was on the special diet list and they thought I couldn't have black pepper. What was going on, they wondered. I wondered also. Was that really me, saying I loved black pepper?

On the other hand, it may simply be getting used to the taste. Love can easily become a habit, can easily lose its energy. My experience with black pepper has shown me how easy it is to take the experiment for the goal rather than the means toward that goal. It's easy to forget that the reason for my experiments that summer was not about black pepper or the heat. How to remember the reason for these experiments, perhaps the reason for being alive?

Feeling myself to be a small piece of this immense world, I feel kinship with every other living thing. In these experiments, I have learned to love even smaller pieces of the world—including the look, the texture, the taste of black pepper.

Jazz

For me, trying to understand what's happening is one of the best ways to get through a difficult experience. Trying to see the difficulty from all sides usually helps. But, difficult experiences have many levels; restless boredom is surely one of the most trying for me. It's not often that boredom overcomes me at the weekly concerts I attend at the Arts & Letters Club, but recently I found myself at a performance by a professional jazz musician, playing both original works and jazz standards, and playing them well. I was restless and a little bored but it gave me the opportunity to try to understand my inability to like this kind of music, and I thought there was a possibility, even in a small, beginner's way, to learn to like what I didn't care to hear—in this instance, jazz.

In present time, my thoughts went something like this: At this particular afternoon concert, I find myself thinking about all kinds of music as we wait for the performer. I'll be attempting to learn how to hear the meaning and sense of jazz, and even to love it as I do classical music, and I wonder why it's been so difficult for me.

Jazz may not be very different from Middle Eastern music or Indian raga, which I like and which I can "hear" and appreciate. They are all mostly improvised and improvised using principles and guidelines. Listening to and appreciating a great musician like Hamza el Din improvise on the *oud* or a musician/scholar of Indian music play a series of improvisations on the *sitar* should be no different from listening right now to this very accomplished jazz pianist improvise or play some of his compositions. He's good. He has a Master's degree in music and is a professor at the university here in Toronto. He has played all over the world and won many awards, and as he begins, I notice that he plays the piano effortlessly and intelligently.

After deciding that improvisation might give us reminders of the act of creation—as it is brought to life—I try to listen more carefully. The pianist begins to play a lovely piece called *Drifters*, which moves away and toward, drifting away and returning back again to its central theme. It has echoes of Chopin in its transparency as well as Adams and Glass as the rhythmic repetitions begin to create a resonance of overtones. It is lovely.

Next there's a piece with many rhythms playing with each other the way two spoon-players or throat-singers might lead and tease each other. Is he improvising? Maybe, although he may have begun from familiar territory, and he's probably played this piece many times before.

Then, the program becomes more serious, more *composed*, and we hear some music by George Gershwin—one of the *Preludes* followed by a version of *Rhapsody in Blue*. Gershwin's music seems to vibrate with a love of jazz. At that time in the musical history of the United States, he was surrounded by the sounds of it. But he surely must have had other influences. For the first time, I notice hints of Rachmaninoff in *Rhapsody in Blue* along with all its jazzy beats.

Trying to understand the purpose of improvisation, and jazz improvisation in particular, it comes to me that all creative enterprises begin with a formal idea—sometimes quite structured, sometimes not. I now begin to recognize some of the harmonies and the particular uses of syncopation and modulations from key to key that may be related to the principles or the formal basis of jazz. It may be that it's this particular form, this "sound" of jazz that I don't understand and therefore, it falls uselessly on my deaf ears. All the great composers have used syncopation and modulation. There are moments of modulation in Mozart's and Schubert's works so perfectly timed that shivers run up my spine every time I hear that momentary shift, and their use of syncopation is subtle and to the point. It's true of all the greats, Beethoven and Hayden as well. And I love their music.

Sometime during the concert I know it is time to get serious, and stop thinking and start listening—and I listen, trying not to be bored and trying to allow something of the pianist's intention to touch me. The harmonies and the rhythms are no different from what I have heard and avoided before—it is still jazz—but I am beginning to listen to the *wholeness* of it, and hear it with another, quieter, more relaxed way of listening. I have experienced this kind of listening before and want to remember to find it again. Surely this more open listening, in any circumstance, might allow understanding to begin, and the beginning of understanding—that miraculous blend of *what I am* and *what I know*—might be the beginning of love.

Note: This chapter was reconstructed from notes and memory after the original was left on a plane going to Philadelphia. That's when I learned a good travel lesson. Check the seat pocket before you leave the plane.

Music

When I'm feeling too busy and forget to rest, it's easy for dark feelings to creep in. This is not good for me or for anyone around me because those dark feelings tend to obscure—and exclude—what I really love. Remembering this now, and remembering the precious qualities that get left out, I want to remind myself that music is one of the joys of my life. I already love music and have always loved music; now, I need to love music *more*.

From my earliest years, music has been one of the most important parts of my life. Listening to music has created many precious, memorable moments of love accompanied by presence and joy—moments of transcendence, one of the finest levels of love. It has taught me wordlessly and patiently. But in no longer listening to music, or playing it often, I've lost something. I need to remember all it has given me and know what is true—I need music in my life.

Many of my deepest memories, still so alive, are about music. One of my earliest memories is of my mother holding me and singing as we moved back and forth in a big rocking chair. I especially loved hearing her sing "Red Sails in the Sunset," which was my favorite. She had an intriguing picture on her bedroom wall, a gift from her first employers, Mr. and Mrs. Winfield, whose stationery store also sold sheet music and records. The Winfields treated my mother like a daughter and after her marriage continued to give her books, music, and pictures. Several of my earliest books—my favorites were *Animal Babies* and *Peter Pan*—were their gifts. One of the pictures they gave her still hangs on my own bedroom wall. It shows an exotic landscape mostly painted in red, an ocean and an ocean-side pond, with red dashes over the pale water—not flamingoes, and not anything definable, but to a young child, looking like red sails.

I was no prodigy, no musical genius, but I had some talent, and music was always important to me. My mother was my first teacher. I began to play the piano and learned to read music when I was four or five. Mostly I remember the long fold-out card tucked behind the keys, with letters and lines showing the piano keys and their names, with Middle C in familiar *safe* territory, in the middle, and extending higher and lower to keys that always felt like another country to me. I remember the almost muscular effort of attention it took to see notes on a page and play those notes on the piano without looking at my fingers on the keyboard. But there are not many memories of those piano lessons, just those two impressions. Later on, there were violin lessons and much better music.

There was a time when I began to hear music telling me stories without words or pictures. As a young child, it seemed to me that music told me things about life, and described feelings and qualities very difficult to put into words; it certainly evoked deep feelings in me. Later, music became a vehicle carrying meaning as well as feeling, and also it brought me a kind of understanding that could be shared.

There are many strong memories from those early years. I still remember myself there, feeling a kind of astonishment when my third grade school teacher played a recording of *The Swan of Tuonela* by Sibelius. It was the first time I heard such music—for me there was no doubt that I was hearing both serenity and sadness communicated by the music. It was also the first time that I was aware of the fact, amazing to a seven-year old, of many different musical instruments with individual voices, each with its own sound yet part of a beautiful wholeness.

If consciousness creates memory, and I believe it does, then I have been touched by consciousness many times when listening to music. I still remember the first time I heard Sibelius' *First Symphony* on the radio and the first time I heard a recording of Brahms' *Double Concerto,* or the afternoon when four of us crowded into a listening booth at the record shop to hear Debussy's *Iberia* for the third or fourth time—I believe we may have worn down those records badly. And, there were many, many more moments like this. Hearing for the first time a recording of Mahler's *Fourth Symphony* with Klemperer and Schwarzkopf. An evening of poetry, music, and Chianti with a group of young would-be bohemians, all of us shocked into silence by Beethoven's *Ninth Symphony*. An epiphany on hearing Mozart's use of syncopation and chromatics.

I have learned substantial lessons from music, such as the time Andre Watts and the San Francisco Symphony performed Bartok's last piano concerto. It was a wondrous performance. I still remember sitting in the balcony of the old San Francisco Opera House, hearing this concerto for the first time, and hearing something *beyond beauty*. It was as if Bartok's voice came through the music, speaking about life itself, describing what life means with all its beauty and with all its pain and difficulties. Yes, he was saying, all of that is true, but beyond the beauty and suffering, what we call life is simply a stream of light and color, and each of our lives is just a particle of this stream. Only later did I read that Bartok wrote that concerto at the end of his sometimes difficult life, sitting in his sick bed—in fact, his death bed—composing a concerto to leave behind for his pianist wife.

I have had similar experiences when listening to the piano music that Gurdjieff wrote with Thomas de Hartmann. Not always, but when it is played by someone practiced in this music, a wordless meaning is expressed in the music they wrote. Sometimes what I hear in this music is simply a description of life, its joys and beauties and the challenges one faces in trying to unlock its secrets, or an echo of traditional folk songs. More rarely the music speaks of worlds beyond our world—worlds with laws, hierarchies, degrees, levels, and movements of energy that no words can accurately describe.

Several years ago at the end of a few days of intensive work with friends in Colorado, I heard someone play one of these remarkable pieces of music. All the conditions were right. The audience was very still, the pianist very attentive, and the intelligence and meaning in the music evoked other worlds. At the same time it was as if I heard Gurdjieff himself speaking. "There's this," he said, as he gestured with his right hand toward the life on earth all around us. "There's this," he said, and gestured with his left hand toward more of the same life on earth. "And there's this," he said, as he looked up and raised both arms straight up toward the heavens. "And here we are," he said, as he moved his head forward and lowered his arms to his sides. I have tried these gestures saying the words to myself when I'm alone. Even without music, practicing them is a help.

Several years ago we were staying near Philadelphia with friends, and one evening, a young woman played one of the Gurdjieff/de Hartmann piano pieces. I had seen this person struggling during the day to understand the personal agendas that seem to get in the way of our working and living closely with other people. Maybe those struggles were a kind of payment in advance because she played very well. As she played, once again I had a glimpse of another world—a world of energies—it was an experience similar to one from a few weeks earlier in Boulder, Colorado. After a time of very quiet work together, I asked someone to play a Gurdjieff/de Hartmann hymn. On both occasions a *fact* about love became clear to me. It was the same fact that I'd experienced before—a fact that started me on this way of learning to love. This is what it says in words: love is a very fine energy that showers down on us at every moment, although we are not always aware of it. Perhaps this fine energy needs human beings who can welcome it and are waiting to receive it. Perhaps this energy needs human beings who can pass it on through color or geometry, music or words, or through their very presence.

Since moving to Toronto, music has given me help and support. I have attended many fine concerts in this city. I have heard Schubert and Schumann expressing their love of life and their fear of loss, the coherence and crystalline certainty of Bach, the sheer joy and beauty of Granados and Villa-Lobos. I have taken *Winter Morning Walks* with Dawn Upshaw, faced the challenge of Bartok's wit and wisdom with the Tokyo String Quartet, and welcomed a new woman composer in *Love From Afar*. When I am able to listen closely to music played with intelligence and passion by brilliant performers—and I've heard quite a few—it's as if the music is in the process of being re-created, newly made. Then I know why I want to learn to love music even *more*, and know why this is possible. The love of music simply needs to be reawakened from its sleep in an almost forgotten place, and awakened more often.

This love has brought me joy and come close to healing some of my anxieties over the years—it has also been a good teacher. Loving music has taught me as much about the meaning of life as any great books. And in listening to music as well as in playing music—alone, in an orchestra, a string quartet or with an accompanist—each time I am reminded of what I already know and asked to listen in new ways: not being taken away by thoughts or dreams, needing to be present and attentive, and simply to listen.

How to remember all of this? Feeling distracted and too busy at home, I can be grateful when my schedule opens up to concerts or I am alone and can listen to music at home or in the car or when I sit down at the piano or open my violin case, take out bow and violin and play a little. I need to find—and never forget—the part of me who is not busy. Something tells me now that this part may also be the one who loves music. Remembering what I love, and learning to love it *more*—this may be the answer to all my questions.

Coda

I have discovered a new symphony.

Some years ago, rather than taking food to an annual New Year's Day brunch, I decided to take a bowl of little folded slips of paper with fortunes written on them—like those in fortune cookies—and to share them with everyone at the brunch. A young friend along with my daughter and young granddaughter Anne helped me write the fortunes. There were good fortunes, crazy fortunes, and some that were just plain silly. I don't remember who received which fortune all those years ago, except for one. Later, a dear friend told me what she read on her slip of paper that day, and how it came true. Her fortune? "*You will get what you wish for.*" That very afternoon of the brunch, after everyone had left, the man she lived with asked her to marry him. That was her wish and it came true. Their marriage was one of the enviable ones. They were very well suited, always happy, always creative, and hosted many more New Year's Day brunches. Privately, I took credit!

I didn't take a slip from the bowl that day, but I knew the one I wanted. My young friend had written, "*You will discover a new symphony.*" What a delightful fortune! And now, it's come true. I have found a new "symphony." It's a symphonic suite called *Kullervo* by Sibelius, one of the first composers to awaken my love for music. I listened to this new symphony for the second time the first day I discovered it, and many times since then. Each time I hear it, I wonder how anyone could doubt that love showers goodness down on us all the time, whether we are composers, or symphony musicians, or listeners. Whether we notice or not.

Sitting Quietly

For many years now, sitting in the morning quietly and alone has been a daily activity. But I don't want this practice to become automatic. I want to feel its importance again—and to love it more.

"Why don't you just sit down and be quiet for a while," a friend suggested by phone in the summer of 1961—when long distance phone calls from New York City were rare and expensive. We had been talking about how I could get through some life difficulties at that time, and his suggestion seemed like a good idea. So I went downstairs to the basement bedroom where there was a big comfortable round-armed chair that had been replaced by the new couch and matching chair upstairs. I'd often used this same old chair to read in, with my legs over one arm and my back against the other. It was a chair with a history of favorite books and crackers and buttermilk snacks, a place of retreat in the middle of life, so it seemed like my friend's good idea would be even better in this chair. I sat down and straightening my arms with my hands on the arms of the chair, lifted my body up high enough to cross my legs under me. The chair was just the right width to allow my knees to stay raised slightly while my ankles were crossed. I don't remember where my hands were, but my back was upright against the back of the chair. I closed my eyes. And there I was. Sitting quietly.

What were my inner experiences during that first intentional sitting? As I recall there were few inner experiences as such. What I tried was not to think and just be there. Trying that rather intensively while sitting in this new posture, was enough to occupy thirty minutes or so of time. In fact, it was a surprise to see how long I sat there.

Many years have passed, and almost every morning I sit alone on a cushion, trying to find silence and awareness of my body. And I ask myself now whether this helps anyone else and what I receive. For the first time now, I want to write down some answers to this question.

Sitting quietly every day gives me a kind of stability and trust in endurance, persistence, and remembrance. This practice has given me a degree or two of self-knowledge and therefore, a broader knowledge of the world. I have had new perceptions and notice that along with the development and nurturing of my own will, there is a greater possibility of truly serving others as well as serving something very much higher than ordinary life—or so I hope when I feel, and know, that my being here on this cushion is important. Simply responding to the need to sit down and be quiet gives me a daily reminder that my wished-for growth of being might be possible after all—especially when the resistance to sitting down and to this growth is seen, and I've seen a lot of resistance.

Lately I've taken Suzuki Roshi's advice. "To take the posture is itself to have the right state of mind," he said. What this means for me is that I need to understand what the posture *is*, as well as what it's for and how to take it. I need to *be* the posture. Many Buddhist methods have entered into the daily practice of many versions of what is called meditation. Mostly, I prefer to find my own way, but Suzuki Roshi's simplicity has sometimes been a guide. This simple bit of advice has provided years of study.

My teacher's guidance to me was even more simple. Lord Pentland told me, "Sit quietly and work." "What do you mean by work?" I asked, and he looked at me with such scorn that I was sorry to have asked. His face told me that this was something I should know by now. I suffered a bit. Then he answered. He gave me no definition and described no method, but paused, thought, and finally said, "Work is standing in a muddy field with only one galosh." End of discussion. But I received a *koan* that has fueled deeper and deeper questions over many years.

Of course, I took other indications he gave, ways that he worked or sat or stood, and many hints, such as the need for relaxation, verticality, and inner silence, and added them to my practice. Also, over the years he gave unique inner exercises to be used along with "sit quietly and work." These exercises have given me a great deal of practice, more information about myself and the world, a deepening understanding of Gurdjieff's ideas, and a direct experience of the greatness that is the source of everything.

Why do we sit upright, rather than lying down in a more relaxed position when we seek to find inner quiet and transcend ordinary life? We are uniquely human when we are vertical, as many scientific studies of ancient humans have shown. Scientists continue to build on this idea in order to place it accurately within evolutionary development of life on earth. But behind the theories, there is an idea: *As above, so below.*

This aphorism has been used for centuries to remind human beings of their place in the universe. It is an open doorway to real knowledge—knowledge both of self and the immense universe we live in. If this is a true statement and more than a simple analogy—Gurdjieff implies that it is both—then it is through studying and understanding ourselves that we can study and understand the cosmos. Taking this as an original truth, a basic, foundational method, toward understanding our world can bring new meaning on many different levels: microscopic, societal, cosmic, and personal.

When I sit on my cushion, quiet and relaxed, aware of my verticality, there are moments when my own presence is clear. Then my awareness is very different from the awareness that mostly serves in my day-to-day life—although more often now there are fewer differences. Now, the finer awareness appears more often in daily living.

Somehow, in ways not easily explained, I find a larger feeling accompanying these moments. Sometimes I am *present* and the whole of existence is also present. When I feel the movement in the channels in my body that transport energies up and down, for a moment I feel a source that has no source. Like Seamus Heaney's "current so in flood it overspills," a new energy enters my body, moving downward and spreading out to the smaller tributaries that nourish the whole organism so well.

Always though, it is necessary to begin with the quiet. My largest experiences haunt me as much as my little failures—they all start the mind working. Together they engage the unnamed part of me that rouses easily and always wants action. In the quiet, that part can find a new role.

More often now I feel a new compassion for the part of me that has collected and remembered so much, who tries to keep things straight and reminds me of what has gone before and what needs to be done—this part wants and needs action. I feel a new respect for that valiant, unappreciated part now, and respect and compassion are essential. After the moment of recognition, they are the first steps toward love, and this part of me is in great need of love. In seeing it more closely, I have understood more deeply that every living thing has a great need for love, even those parts that seem to hold me prisoner.

Working to relax sounds contradictory, yet without work and constant awareness relaxation quickly disappears. I need to remember myself and what I want. Then the attention that results from inner work can help the relaxation to be steadier, which allows the sensation of my body to take its place. This sensation lives underneath the tension. In fact, a whole inner world exists there. I need to remember that and try to keep the door open to both this inner world and to the world around me. I need to find a breathing space where the flow of thoughts and desires slows down for a moment. When it pauses, there is space and I can receive something new—a glimpse of the unknown world I call myself as well as the outer world in all its magnificence: trees, sky, grass, stone, wood. There is stillness in the pause, and quiet, with no apparent movement—yet at the same time, there is radiating life. To experience the *moment between moments* and the deep relaxation that results is worth every payment one has made, or that might be yet to come.

Now, many years after that first time I sat alone in my parents' basement, my feeling about sitting has changed. It is a feeling closer to the neutrality and inclusiveness of love. I am more and more impressed by both the mystery of sitting and the facts it shows me—my body is a living, breathing organism, and at the same time it is a feeling, thinking organism, and I am a human being who sometimes hears a whisper from within that tells me: *Wake up. Remember who you are.*

Early Mornings

It's summer in Colorado. The quiet outside is early-morning quiet. Just now at 7 a.m., it's very still, although as I listen, there are a few faint sounds: in the distance an airplane and a dog barking; closer to the patio, a bird in the big tree; a little farther away beyond the garage, a group of birds all speaking at the same time. The light is cool. All the greens are more blue than yellow, although yellow-green dapples glisten in the leaves of the trees on the other side of the footpath at the bottom of the property.

Already the sun is warming the building next to us and changing its appearance, creating a sharp division between the washed-out warmth that has almost no color and the still-cool shadow side that is a cool brown, a cool mysterious brown. Watching the line of color illuminated by the sun as it moves to the north on the wall, I can see and feel the inevitable heat that will surround us later in the morning. Already it's warmer upstairs than down and I've already shut the upstairs windows, closed the south-facing curtains.

How good it is to have this time, this early morning time. It's good to be part of the awakening of light and warmth, to watch the color of the wall across the yard slowly fade under the unstoppable pressure of the sunlight. "Inexorable," as Professor Syzmanski at Western State College used to say, "which means it can't be prayed out of." Nothing or no one can stop this gradual enlightening. It's the movement of time itself, which turns the tides and dims the light, and cools the heat, and now, is visibly warming the earth, the trees, the wall of the building next to us, and changing the colors as it warms.

Isn't it better to experience this, I ask myself. Better than sleeping away the morning hours, trying to make up for sleep time missed the night before. It's time for being alone, and I want a certain amount of solitude. I need to arrange this, to choose it more often.

Now, I come face to face with important clues about the learning process: intention, aim, and choice. I went to bed early last night and got up early this morning. And now I can feel how it is to be here alone, letting the early morning sounds and colors touch me, as I intended.

Once again, the profusion of the letter "I" in my writing strikes me. Should this be troublesome, or not? Perhaps it's not egotism but an affirmation, and necessary. In learning how to love, no matter what the object of that love is, there must be a subject, a person who loves. The learning itself, along with the wish to learn must come from me—and from no one else. I make a plan. I get up early. Yes. And because of my plan and my response to the plan, I am able to sit here alone as the early morning slowly changes colors and temperature.

Having faced this worry, I can return to what's happening now and begin to feel the depth of it. Begin to feel the silence of it. The silence is there under the sounds of a car in the street outside and the less frequent sounds of the birds, already getting ready for the heat, folding up the instruments they used to announce the light. It's under everything, this silence. Under, above, around.

I stop writing for a moment and realize that listening to the sound of the pen on the paper is not a distraction but a joy, and the silence touches my heart more deeply. I say my *heart* for lack of a better word. All of me—heart, mind, and body—feels this.

The silence asks me to be here in its world, to stop and be myself. It invites me to be here within the beauty of sound and sight while a whisper of cool air from the open north-facing door touches my legs and face. A line from the *Arabian Nights* comes to mind: *I hear and I obey*.

Later, after sitting quietly for half an hour, I stand up refreshed, which means the reawakening of my interest. This interest is not quite curiosity or wanting to know more. It is being open to something new.

From that openness, and having a little early morning time left over, I sit down to look at the big Oriental rug book, *From Timbuktu to Tibet*, from an exhibit fueled and funded by textile-lovers, collectors of rugs and tapestries who live in New York City. These men and women have collected, studied, and shared these precious examples of weaving, which so strongly demonstrate the human need, capacity, and longing for beauty. That it's not just any beauty is evidenced by the variety and splendor of the designs from which the textiles are born. If nature loves variety, and surely she does, these textiles collected from around the world are in close competition with the natural world for both beauty and creativity. In fact they may be *more* natural—more appealing to the nature of us human beings—because they reveal an underlying design, whether intricate or simple, that is more difficult to perceive in nature.

What a joyful early morning it's been. Filled with impressions from many sources: light, sound, temperature, color and design, strong tea, and at the end of my time alone, a good talk with my husband about Light and Life as likened to Mind and Soul in an old translation of the *Hermetica*.

Now I know more about what it is to love the early morning hours that begin at the magical moment of first light, just before sunrise, and end when the work day begins. Today, I have felt the quality of these early morning hours. It has the taste of an open invitation and I have felt welcomed.

Today, I know what it is to love early mornings. It's only one morning, just a beginning, and there is much more to understand, but the feeling can remember, and the mind and also the body. Now, it's about remembering. Remembering myself feeling delight and joy in hearing the sounds and seeing the sights this morning. Remembering silence and how the word *Hermetica* resonated with the meaning of Mind and Soul, remembering the taste of tea, the soft sensation of cool air, the color of heat on a wall, and so much more. Remembering to give my attention freely, sensing and feeling the silence and sights and sounds, the temperatures and textures of early morning. And always, remembering my own presence, as well. All this must surely be my entry into more early mornings—wherever I am—welcoming what appears, with love.

Solitude

In my life now, solitude is not about being alone or about loneliness. Although I often feel lonely, I am seldom alone. The late hours of the day and the very early ones sometimes allow me to be alone, to feel more of my own energy within the quiet in the apartment, and right or wrong, those times of being alone are my choice. But, what I wish for is not created by being alone in the world or finding ways to heal my loneliness; it's about understanding and loving what I am *inside,* beyond all that.

Loneliness has appeared and reappeared throughout my life. As I look at it now, it seems less about physical distances from others and more about wanting to be close to those who value me and actually see me and listen as I try to say what's in my mind and heart. There have been many lonely moments in my life—sometimes in a group of casual friends, sometimes with someone who couldn't or wouldn't see me.

But also, I am lonely without my family and close friends. With several exceptions in Toronto, friends for whom I am very grateful, almost all my family and friends live in the United States and most of them live in the western states. Each year now, within my family and circle of friends, there are new marriages, new babies, people growing older, people getting sick, and people dying—all creating new demands to travel. When I visit, so much is given to me. It's as good for me as it is for a grandchild to go to the mall together, have lunch, and shop—the difference being that now she drives and I am the passenger. How wonderful it is to hold a baby born a few hours earlier. How relaxing it is just to watch a movie or a sitcom with my daughter and her husband, or walk in Golden Gate Park. This is when I know that presence itself is what is most important. Just being with my loved ones helps me in very many ways, but most of all, they remind me of our human *beingness*, and I love them even more for that.

I miss my family and friends; that is very true. But more than that, I also miss a specific kind of group meeting, an exchange of ideas and experiences with other people that can only happen after many years of working together.

From the beginning of my life in San Francisco, there were always others to work with. Not everyone is still alive now and not everyone still lives and works in San Francisco, but there are still many of us who recognize each other when I visit the Bay Area—the members of the Gurdjieff Foundation that my sister and I were part of since 1961. Even though it's been more than a few years since I left San Francisco, after so many years of meeting weekly to exchange the results of inner work, along with frequent meetings to plan work events together, I still feel the absence of my peers, my *people*, all related by a common line of work.

Since leaving San Francisco, several contradictions in my life have become more and more apparent. I travel a lot, but not very often to the West Coast. I miss being with friends and family, but need to be alone to recuperate and catch my breath—even phone calls take too much from me. When the demands of the household slow down or in the days between travels, I often feel lonely, yet the feeling of loneliness alternates with simply needing some empty space.

My time alone is now more valuable than it's ever been. I want to find my own tempo, to be able to be quiet and relaxed, to be able to ponder and try to think clearly enough to write something with meaning. When I'm not too tired, the latest and the earliest hours can be good for this. It was during these times that the true meaning of solitude came to me.

As I tried to look more directly at my understanding and experience of loneliness and of "aloneness," I began to recognize a third quality. This is a unique taste of solitude, different in several ways from either loneliness or a recuperative need to be alone. First of all, it is never negative; solitude has no sadness or longing. On the contrary, the feeling of solitude seems to belong to a group of what I call positive emotions, such as gratitude or acceptance, which differ from their ordinary cousins that use the same names. A positive emotion is rare and seldom appears on its own. Although it can come as a gift of grace, it is most often, in my experience, the result of effort—a particular voluntary effort of attention. Such an emotion is either present or not—it has no opposite, unlike ordinary emotions, which can become their opposite in an instant. And, living in solitude means living in the present moment with no longing or regret for anything in the past, no fear of the future, but living joyfully—now. In this way, the feeling of solitude is very similar to the feeling of *love*.

In beginning to understand and experience more about solitude, I felt kinship with the Desert Fathers. These men—perhaps women lived this way, too—must also have experienced moments of joy and awareness in their solitude. In my busy life, I am grateful that the ideas I've studied and the help I've been given over the years have allowed me to taste something that perhaps they paid for with privation and complete aloneness. Of course, real solitude has often evaded me, but sometimes it was there, and then—joy.

Gurdjieff said, "Remember yourself always and everywhere." This effort can create a unique experience in which the incessant, almost unrelenting movement outward of my attention pauses and takes one of two directions. In that moment, I can experience something new—new because it is a movement inward, toward myself. At that moment, I am called to see who I am and what I truly want. Then I am alone and at the same time in the world. I often feel the *solitude* of this effort when I simply sit quietly, trying to be relaxed and still, with no aim other than to be present.

Efforts of this kind over the years have deepened my relation to profound silence, a silence that is *not nothing*. In a way, it is *everything*. And, it is never a dull, colorless silence. It is always alive, sparkling with life. I described it once in an unpublished interview in this way: "Silence is not empty. That's why emptiness is not necessarily the best term for it. Real silence has resonance. It's a living thing and it requires a very, very quiet body, a very relaxed mind and body to just perceive the edge of it. Perhaps silence is only a hint. Last week, I perceived it as the *outer edge of God*. Just the outer edge—just a *whisper of God*."

Although the silence of solitude comes to me most often when I sit alone, trying to relax and be still, there are many moments when this same silence appears in the midst of life itself. I try to remember myself, and sometimes the living memory of silence returns and enlivens me. Whether I'm cooking or washing dishes—sometimes even in the midst of a confrontation—behind the external objects and events, there is silence.

I sometimes feel the joy of solitude during a walk through wooded avenues, when I'm listening to music, playing the piano or the violin, or trying to put words together in such a way that it satisfies me, knowing someone else might understand. In these moments, there is real solitude. Then, I am a sole entity alone in a living world, not lonely, and so much closer to being able to love.

Being Loved

Air Canada. Altitude 30,000 feet. Denver to Toronto. I'm flying back to Toronto from a good visit to Colorado. It was a week filled with discovery. New facts and new facets emerged, about me and about others, too. Facts related to the dynamism of a group. Subtle facets of great ideas that illuminated long-standing questions. A new feeling of myself in relation to the group and to the great ideas. It's time to relax a little, even here, so high in the air, going so fast. Soon we'll be landing and I'll need to face the facts and facets of life there in Toronto.

But first, I ask myself, what do I want to learn right now? An answer comes immediately. Some people seem to respect and love me yet it's difficult for me to appreciate or accept that. Could I learn to accept being loved? Accepting the feeling of being loved might help me begin to like this feeling—and eventually, to love being loved.

Now, I find myself on an airplane, returning from a few days of intensive inner work with other people and trying to face something true in myself. Yes, the thought of being loved feels good, but side by side with that thought, there is another thought that voices a very small feeling about being *unworthy*. It's hidden and mostly unvisited. What is the next step out from that? Thinking about how often I've felt not quite able to accept love or respect—there have been too many moments like that—I begin to think about what being unworthy means to me. And

I see myself as a very small, colorless, unnoticeable thing, not quite a person—not worthy of anyone's noticing me or acknowledging my existence—or recognizing any of my needs.

Then, another thought and another feeling come into view. Too often I think of myself not only as unworthy, but also as *undeserving* because I haven't paid enough—haven't worked hard enough, haven't proved myself sufficiently intelligent, haven't given enough time or energy to others—and the full, sufficient payment seems always out of reach. Feeling undeserving seems to be about doing—sometimes about not doing something, sometimes about doing the wrong thing, almost always about not doing enough. I feel unworthy when I see myself as a truly insignificant, unimportant person, and undeserving when I've not earned love or respect. I am unworthy and never do enough. Being and doing, doing and being—the two poles of human existence—sometimes manifesting at a very low level, where they continually drag me down; at that level, neither are worth much of anything to someone trying to become a real human being.

Which comes first, what I am or what I do? In life, being and doing are not opposites. They complement each other and one without the other cannot function well or long. In trying to comprehend this, I see a different possibility. On the one hand, when both being unworthy and not doing enough are present and operating together, there is almost no possibility of accepting love. However, there is another level where being and doing are necessary attributes of a real human being. Remembering this helps me remember the possibility of a harmonious relation between being and doing, on a completely different level.

Two forces or vital energies often create a deadly balance or standoff until the whole process fades away or one overpowers the other. A *third* aspect or force is always necessary for harmony, life, and dynamic movement. Is there a third aspect that could create a longer-lasting balance between being and doing, reconciling and making possible a real relationship, elevating them toward harmony? For a moment, I see that there is something like *ableness*, like *being able*, that might be this third aspect. It is certainly different from either being or doing. Being is about being something, in my case, a person and what I am; doing is about action and what I do. For me, being able is about neither. It is readiness, knowledge, the ability to persist, and willingness to be beginning again and again. It is presence.

Could being able be learned or is it the result of learning—not the kind of learning that happens in school or from family or friends or culture, but an intentional learning that becomes a real part of a person for a lifetime, or maybe longer? This learning would come from my own choice and determination. Maybe one finds a *sangha*, a holy community, a teacher, or a teaching. It is my hope for our world that there are still men or women to be found who may be trustworthy guides, those who are teachers themselves or have learned from teachers, or who have also found how to learn for themselves. But maybe at some point, one creates one's own place of learning and charts one's own course. Some of us have had the good fortune to have experienced both these possibilities.

Now, wise words come to me from my inner source of wisdom, words which surely must relate to the triad of being, doing, and being able: *In order to love being loved, you must be a hundred times more relaxed. In order to love another person, you must be even more relaxed than that.*

But it's time to walk and keep the blood flowing in my legs. Walking up and down the aisle, I'm aware of the plane, flying thousands of feet above the ground and moving at least 500 miles per hour. While we are moving so fast, at such an altitude, for the most part, the plane's passengers try to pass the time. Some sleep—I try not to intrude on their privacy as I go down the aisle—and many watch the video screens, a few read books.

Images come to me of airplanes, satellites, armies, explosions, tall heavy buildings, billions of cars, sound waves, internet signals—and so, on and on—that cover our world, and hide it from us. Mostly, we don't really see it or recognize it as a living being. But our world, this planet Earth, surely is worthy of love and deserves being loved. Surely, it is able to receive whatever attention and love we can give. It might even love being loved in a way that is beyond our comprehension. Can we human beings, so adept at finding ways to pass the time, notice and acknowledge this great being on which we live, and learn to love it—and each other?

Pondering this question, I return to my seat. My seat mate looks up from her book and turns to look at me. She gives me a big, welcoming smile. I feel the warmth of her smile and smile back. I am more relaxed—not a hundred times more relaxed, but relaxed enough to accept her welcome. No words are exchanged, but something else passes between us. *We see each other*. I know that my questions are answered in that moment. They will come again, but for now, no words are necessary. Just now, feeling both worthy and deserving, I'm learning how to be able to give—and to receive—love.

"Any prayer may be heard by the Higher Powers and a corresponding answer obtained only if it is uttered thrice: Firstly—for the welfare or the peace of the soul of one's parents. Secondly—for the welfare of one's neighbor. And only thirdly—for oneself personally."

–G.I. Gurdjieff

My Parents

My quiet sittings in the morning usually begin as Gurdjieff suggested. This ritual has become increasingly important, and without it, I feel that something is missing. It helps me in several ways. At this stage of life, I need to feel that I'm helping others, trying to give something back to my parents even now, and trying to help all my neighbors—including my daughters and their families and my husband and his family and all the billions of people who attempt to make their lives on this difficult but beautiful planet. It's not always about helping others though; sometimes, without waiting to ask for my own welfare, when my need is too great, I first ask all these dear ones to help me—and I feel that they do.

In beginning this series of experiments in learning to love, I was convinced that in order to love someone, or something, it is necessary first to *see* them. Everyone and everything wants to be seen. The trees and mountains, the lake and golden meadows—when I really look at them, they respond in the fullness of life, as if they have been waiting for someone to see them. It's the mystery of life. Nothing exists alone, without relationship. Recognition and acknowledgement of the *other* nourish and heal. And we can benefit by taking our place in life. We are real human beings only when we are conscious and aware with our vision unclouded by judgment, and we become even *more* human when we are aware and also feel love and delight for all living things.

After my father died, I tried to remember his face. I studied pictures of him when he was young—a little boy with light blue eyes. I looked closely at pictures of him as a young man, holding me when I was a little baby with blue eyes and dark hair just like his. I studied pictures of him as an older man, but mostly they brought little feeling. Finally several events brought him back to me.

In the year after his death, I was troubled almost every day by loneliness. I missed my father and at that time, I had few male friends. My daily life became so painful that one afternoon I simply went to my cushion and sat down, feeling desperate and knowing I needed help. I thought first of my father and wondered, *Could I ask him to help me?* No, I thought, remembering our differences—but just then something new occurred to me. Everything has changed, I thought, things are different now. Our relationship—who he was, who I was—all of this has changed. Now my father is free of all the personal attributes, the criticism and sarcasm, the wry way with words—everything that kept me from asking his advice when he was alive. Now I could ask, and now he could help.

Silently, I explained my situation and asked him to help me if he could. Almost immediately, my whole body relaxed. I felt very quiet and very calm—for me, it was a miracle. And miraculously, within days my life took a turn for the better.

A few years later, I dreamed about my father. It was one of those special never-to-be-forgotten dreams, which happen rarely in a lifetime. Very early one morning my cat, Demi, motivated perhaps by one of his peculiar notions or simply serving good fortune—or magic—jumped up onto my bed, climbed onto my chest, and breathed into my face until he woke me up at just the right moment. I opened my eyes at the very moment I was actively dreaming about my father and a conversation we'd had about fifteen years earlier, which I'd forgotten. In the dream, he and I were standing on our back porch, which was glassed in and quiet. The light was summery. I saw the scene very clearly and even remembered some details. I'd been reading about Gurdjieff that year in P.D. Ouspensky's book, *In Search of the Miraculous*, and as I stood there, talking with my father, I was trying to follow Gurdjieff's advice to remember myself. With beginner's luck, in trying this "remembering myself," I was very present that day, and as we talked I felt that both of us were present, my father and I.

But in the dream Demi gave me, it wasn't just about my talking to my father while trying to remember myself, and both of us being there together. He was *alive*. I *felt* his life and who he was—felt that mysterious sense of another's presence, which is beyond words and appearances. As I woke up and opened my eyes, the memory lingered of just that—the *feeling* of my father. Even now as I write, I remember the delicate taste of that feeling. I've been able to find it again when remembering my father and later, my mother, after they were gone. This taste of another's presence is what I try to put into place in the little morning ritual that's developed over the years.

For many years, I have often silently repeated what's called the Prayer of the Heart, asking for help and mercy. It appears for me in one of two forms: *Lord, Jesus Christ, have mercy on me.* Or sometimes, *Lord, Jesus Christ, King of the Universe, have mercy on me a sinner.* It depends on the extent and depth of my need.

After I repeat this prayer ten times, I add, "And have mercy on All Creation—especially on my parents, Joseph and Carrie." In saying their names, I try to return to this feeling of each of them, of his presence and hers. That is how my morning ritual begins.

As I've examined many aspects of my life over the last few years, trying to learn to love each one, there have been good results that have added riches to my experiences. For example, sometimes while looking directly at one aspect of my life, additional memories emerge. Previously forgotten but still alive, they touch and animate my feeling, adding fuel to my search and bringing happiness. Here is one of those memories.

When I went into my father's hospital room in Grand Junction before my return to California, for what was to be our final visit, he looked transformed. His face was full of wonder as he told me he'd been in Australia. He added that it was only a dream, but it was clear that for him it was real, he felt he'd been there. No details, just the fact of having been there. His face and his voice told me how amazing this had been for him. He had never been there but I had, and he knew it. And then, as he told me his dream, we had something in common. I can't define it now. I couldn't really put it into words even then. As I sat beside him holding his hand, we shared an experience. He spoke again of being in Australia and I said I'd been there, too. No other words were necessary. Australia—the air and sky, the sounds of birds and people with a strange, sing-song way of talking, the color of the soil and the color of the trees— an experience in common, wordlessly, as if our impressions intermingled.

It's easy now to analyze this event and say that the earlier difficulties we had as father and daughter simply disappeared and that something was healed. But those are just words. Even though they're true, they're just words. What I know now, right now, is that with no words at all we both understood something very high and very important—we were simply alive together. Together we experienced a moment of relation that was so real I felt it could last even beyond death. I hope this is true and that this moment was a help to him when he died a few weeks later—with a smile, the nurse said to my mother. And I pray that what he and I shared will be a help to me as well, sometime in the future, in similar circumstances.

After my father died, my mother and I were blessed with more years in which to deepen our relationship—phone conversations, letters in which she expressed what she called her "deep thoughts," visits to my place and to hers, grocery shopping, wonderful sincere talks, and a road trip from San Francisco to Boulder, Colorado. Once, my younger daughter and I rented a condo for two weeks in Pagosa Springs, also in Colorado, and after we arrived we invited my mother to join us. She immediately and promptly said Yes to our invitation and flew in the next day. On this trip, she was the only one brave enough and strong enough to unhook a little trout one of us caught, and she was the one who without hesitation went to the back of an abandoned cemetery, moved some bushes aside, and found the grave of my father's grandfather.

After selling her big Colorado house, she moved to Spokane, Washington, and later to Sacramento, California, and warmer weather. After her death, which was a remarkable event, I treasured her books, with margin notes she'd written or notes on slips of paper tucked into the pages. She was a beautiful and deeply thoughtful woman, and now I begin to think of her as my first and most important teacher, hoping that some of her strength, will, and practical knowledge has passed down to me. I remember her with gratitude and love.

As the years add up to more and more years and a longer life, as I am a little closer to being a more normal, adult human being, the love I feel for my parents has changed. It is deeper, less personal, and more direct; it begins to resemble *real* love—the kind I've written about in these notes. Now, it is closer to the love that heals, closer to being pure healing energy. I can sincerely say that now I love both my parents equally and fully. I am sure that learning to love them *more* has enabled a broader, deeper love, which can include many others. Wishing to have been a better daughter and feeling the limits of my nature spurs a wish in me to develop real compassion. I wish not to be discouraged by the inconsistencies of my ability to love, which is often stronger one day, weaker another—and I want to continue this practice of learning to love as long as I'm able. Day by day, I am full of thanks for my parents and for their love.

My Neighbor

Christianity, the religion of love. "*Love thy neighbor as thyself.*" "*Love one another, as I have loved you.*" These words strike me right in the center of my life. Can I love my neighbor or anyone else—even my parents, my children or my husband—as commanded in the Gospels?

But, I ponder. Would Christ have asked his followers to love if it was impossible? Surely not. Surely, the disciples who received this teaching must have been able to do it. Why else would he say to them, "Love one another" or "Love your neighbor"? I believe that these men—and surely women also heard and practiced this teaching—were extraordinary to begin with and through their practice developed capacities that we can only imagine now, let alone emulate honestly. Still, two thousand years later we human beings must contain traces of these capacities, and I believe these traces, like carefully tended seeds, can grow.

Almost everyone suggests that we need to love. The Dalai Lama, most religious leaders, and every other article, post, or talk by those who want to help us be better people say the same thing. But few people tell us *how* to love. Now, after several years of experiment and study, I know something about how to love—about loving intentionally.

A willingness to experiment is important and necessary, along with a great deal of work. To acquire the *ableness* to love, the mind, heart, and body all need to be present and more or less in relation to each other;

the attention needs to be free to see and listen, not tangled up with random thoughts and impulses; and the wish to be able to love needs to be strong and relatively pure. It's been my experience that sometimes when my inner world is arranged in these ways—or, on the other hand, sometimes when I wish to do this but realize that I am completely unable—the energy I need is *bestowed*, making it possible to begin. Then, feeling more whole and wishing to be able to love, I find the way toward giving my attention freely and completely to another person, or to a plant or animal, or to the mountains, the lake, and the sky.

Now in writing these words, I find myself again right at the center of my own life, and also at the heart of this book. I'm remembering some of the words, first reported in the preface, that came to me on that sunny, wintery day in Colorado: *It's best to learn to love everything.*

Before beginning this series of experiments, *choosing* to love seemed almost impossible. I had seen love appear in me and felt its warmth move from my heart to all the little edges and spaces of my body, just as I'd felt it go the other direction, moving from the body to the heart and filling it to overflowing. But that was not my doing. Love happened because life arranged it. I loved my children from when they were born, and also my parents more or less since the time I was born. They were *my* children and *my* parents. I loved men when there was intellectual ground and physical attraction in common. And so, on and on it went. In my experience, love was either there or not, and feeling love was not really up to me. But now, over the last few years, starting from my earliest experiment in learning to love the dark, I know another way is possible.

Where to begin? Can I learn to love my neighbor? Maybe I need to ask a very simple question more often—who is my neighbor? And with this question, I can begin where all these experiments have begun—trying to be present and to see someone or something more clearly, in person or in my mind's eye, without judgment or analysis, without being taken by their manifestations, but searching to see simply who or what they are. I resolved to experiment as often as possible in this way, looking at or listening to the people in my life and remembering the simple question, *Who is my neighbor?*

As I watch the woman checking out my groceries or make room for someone to sit next to me on a plane, I ask myself, is this person truly my neighbor? During lunch with a friend—is she my neighbor? Can I *see* her? Can I *listen* as I try to stay open to someone's voice on the phone? Can I *hear* him?

Recently a friend and I met for lunch. We don't get together often—she lives in Colorado; I live most of the year in Toronto. So we had a lot of catching up to do. It took three hours! But what a good time we had. Our being together gave me opportunity after opportunity to try to remember that I was there, listening, and trying to see *her*. As we both tried to put some of our deeper feelings into words, I became more and more aware that both of us were there. A profound experience, as I repeatedly relaxed and listened and watched—and tried not to be overwhelmed by the love I felt for her, and at the same time for everyone and everything.

For me now, much of my questioning and searching to understand, my wish to be myself—all this is part of what Gurdjieff described as a Fourth Way or a work in life, and I try to take advantage of the many opportunities life gives me. But the necessity for a daily quiet work has become increasingly important. My quiet sittings in the morning usually begin as Gurdjieff suggested, asking "Firstly—for the welfare or the peace of the souls of one's parents. Secondly—for the welfare of one's neighbor. And only thirdly—for oneself personally." When I first began this practice, I asked first for the welfare of both my parents along with two spiritual teachers who have been like parents, and then, when asking for the welfare of my neighbors, I pictured all my immediate family followed by my close friends.

Since those beginning years, the boundary of my neighborhood has expanded greatly. Today, in my morning prayers I continue to ask for mercy—that sacred energy—to rain down on all creation, and especially on my neighbors. The list of my neighbors now includes close family members, my husband and his family, close friends, especially those with serious health challenges or who have just passed on to another world, and individuals in Gurdjieff groups all over the world. At some point, this prayer for mercy expands to include also all of humanity, especially those who are hungry, homeless, frightened, despairing, grieving, and perhaps most important, all those with violence in their hearts. It's a big neighborhood and it takes some time to move around it, trying to *see* and *feel* all these human beings—trying to see their faces in my mind's eye, feeling how they live, the joys and sorrows they bear, and acknowledging the radiant wish for goodness and happiness at the center of life itself.

Feeling who they are, all my neighbors, I sometimes feel who I am too, as I did with my friend. Then, when there are two of us, *love* appears, and for a moment, something new comes into being. We experience this new entity as *relationship*, a trinity created by the energy we call love. Even though it's momentary, the feeling of relationship, the feeling of love, remains in my innermost memory and reminds me not to forget a certain truth: it's *always* possible to "love my neighbor as myself." Being able to remember is what I wish for myself *personally*.

My Companion

All of us human beings are always relating, always in relation to something. Something far away or something close by. Something good for us or not so good, and so on. Within this embracing movement toward someone or something other, many of us find companions—other human beings we want to be with. Of course, some people relate better to animals or to their plants or to their jobs, or their god, but all around the world, many of us find another person who seems to be the one. And then we try to live with that person. It seems quite natural, yet it's not always easy.

Human beings are not easy to love—other emotions get in the way. Even babies can make a parent feel self-pity or resentment, and adults can be even more difficult than children to live or work with. There are many ways another person can offend me or go against what I want or believe. Yes, human beings are difficult to love. They are quirky, changeable, and too often unreliable. They say one thing and do another. Yet in spite of many disappointments—disappointments in myself as well as in other people—I have experienced rare moments of what might be real relationship in my life, moments when the differences and rough edges between me and others disappeared, and we were truly related. These experiences have gradually helped create a wish in me to be able to love other people, and to love more often and more sincerely—by choice rather than by good luck or fortuitous accident.

With my parents and children there have been many moments in which love for them awakened in me, although sadly, this has been too easy to forget in the rush of life. Like many people, I looked for relationships outside the circle of family, and finding these relationships, was sooner or later disappointed even as I hoped for the best. I wanted these relationships to grow and continue beyond the random hazards of life with its short-lived attractions and the pulls of two bodies or the attractions and agreements of two minds. This seldom happened; something was always missing. The relationships formed within a common spiritual practice were more reliable and long-lasting, yet still wanting something, still not reliable *no matter what*, still too dependent on an attitude that had to be maintained. At the same time, all these experiences gave me hope and a motive to go on trying, in spite of disappointments. Finding something more long-lasting in my relations with other people became more and more important.

More often now I feel called to love others by something less easy to describe, something less visible than the outer experiences of life, something that feels like *goodness*, and I believe that this urge I feel toward the good is evidence of a genuine human quality, which all of us may share. If wanting to answer to goodness is true for me, surely it is true for many people. The fact of this call and my ability to hear it makes me more human, a small particle of life whose role and service may be to learn to love other human beings—and all of life.

But as I write, I remember—*love is an energy*. Where does this energy come from? What action on my part helps it come alive in me? It seems to appear by degrees. In the beginning, it's there only for a small, tentative moment when another person is present to me and I see him as if for the first time. This is a special moment, and moments such as this leave a trail of tentative and mysterious markings that I can find again. Remembering the energy itself, both its effect on me and its unique, yet familiar taste, I remember and follow its trace. In this way, I begin to learn how to love this person, this companion, this mate.

Remembering the way—first, see and then, love—I am reminded again that the energy of love, like the energy of consciousness, unites. It is truly unitive. When it is present, it unifies and brings the parts of a human being, the mind, body, and feeling of a person, into relation just as it unites people within a feeling that is no longer completely personal. In this closeness, a real relationship is created, a relationship that is able to contain all the pushes and pulls that inevitably come up between two people. When the energy of love is present, no attitude rearrangements or mental reminders are needed. It unites and lights the way back to the small, tentative but precious moments of presence, again and again. The way becomes clearer and easier to remember, and the substance of love begins to create a kind of container that can hold two people close. With time and practice, more of this special substance is put into place, and the container of relationship grows stronger, holds firm, and can contain even more than two people—the energy of love at its finest is wide enough and deep enough to contain all of life. But the first experiences are small, seemingly accidental or the result of grace. How to learn to love so there are more experiences, more special moments? How to begin?

The best place to begin is always with the truth, to see what is true right now—that I am *not* loving this other person right now. In fact, right now, it is not possible. Something is preventing the magical moment I long for, the moment when another person is present to me and I see him as if for the first time, when the moment is new and the energy of love is present. But I try not to think about what this block is or analyze it. I simply begin with the truth. I am *not* loving this person right now. In fact I may not even be listening or looking at him. I am absent.

When the truth of a situation has quieted me down, I begin to see a little deeper and understand another truth: beyond the difficulties of personality differences, human beings are difficult to love because they are not easy to see. It's easier to begin to learn to love something that is slower, as I did with darkness. Light, dark, the twenty-four hours we say comprise a day—all of this is a different, slower time and easier to study. But people move so fast. They live in streams of time in constant motion, as if their molecules are constantly rearranging as they move along like a swiftly flowing river. To see the whole person, you need to be very patient, and very quiet inside. In that way it is sometimes possible to see the reality of a human being.

Try to find a way to look closely at a person when they're giving their whole attention to something or someone. Or notice the moment when they're between words, or better still, between thoughts, in that wonderful moment when thoughts have failed to supply an answer and only a question remains. If you know them well, find them when they're sleeping—it's not only a sleeping child that catches our hearts. Find your husband sleeping on his side, curled up like a little boy, lost in dreams, or your wife asleep on her back, mouth slightly open and relaxed, vulnerable.

When you find this person in such moments, *see*, just watch. Be very still yourself, in that place between thoughts where there are no answers and not even any questions, where it's easier to see. Then quietly, just look at that person. Begin by simply trying to see *him*, and if you can, try to leave off expectations or memories or wanting anything. Do this often, and almost without noticing that it's happening, you will begin to love him—not who he is, what he does or has done or will do, not any of those things. You will love *him*.

My Enemy

In the beginning, there was the persistent question, what is love? The answer I've come to is simple. Love is an energy. This energy heals, nourishes, and creates relationship and acceptance. When I remind myself that the feelings of being related, of fully accepting the other and of feeling myself as one side of a two-sided equation, which sometimes becomes more than the sum of its parts—a trinity of *relationship*—I know these feelings are surely the result of love. Maybe I could manufacture the same feelings but finally, they would be hollow, pretended feelings, without love. Real love is possible. But it takes work to be able to love. And you have to want it.

Another question about love has arisen in me while writing down my experiences and thoughts about loving other people, such as my companion, my parents, and my neighbors. Is there an additional result, a benefit even, to learning to love that most people might be unaware of? More simply, might there be a hidden or *esoteric* reason for attempting to learn to love?

This question about esotericism came to me when I was looking at what the Gospels had to say about love. The verses about loving one's enemy startled me. What does this mean, I wondered, and looked at more translations. The more recent translations are even more explicit. They all say more or less the same thing: love your enemies because it's difficult; it's easy and unrewarding to love your friends. In other words, anyone can love someone who is similar, a friend, for instance, but it is not easy to love an enemy.

Matthew 5:43-48 Douay version

43 You have heard that it hath been said, Thou shalt love thy neighbour, and hate thy enemy.
44 But I say to you, Love your enemies: do good to them that hate you: and pray for them that persecute and calumniate you.
45 That you may be the children of your Father who is in heaven, who maketh His sun to rise upon the good, and bad, and raineth upon the just and the unjust.
46 For if you love them that love you, what reward shall you have? Do not even the publicans this?
47 And if you salute your brethren only, what do you more? Do not also the heathens this?
48 Be you therefore perfect, as also your heavenly Father is perfect.

In looking at the different translations, and feeling the questions they roused in me, a possible meaning came to me. Perhaps Christ was asking his followers to do the most difficult thing, *love your enemy*, not because it was the "right" thing to do, not because it was the morally correct thing to do, but because attempting to do this would by necessity develop an almost unused and undeveloped part of them—their will—and in turn, create real love. Perhaps something else might be developed as well, something new, which could both contain and manifest love. He knew that in order to face what is difficult, almost impossible, work is necessary. A part of oneself must relax and open, be aware, think, feel, act if necessary. In order to face what is difficult intentionally, all this—the relaxation, the opening, the awareness that arises from this part must be *exercised* or practiced repeatedly, toward an aim of development. Some would say, toward the development of a soul.

Here is another translation of Mathew 5:46, ". . . if you love only those who love you, what reward have you earned?" And another: "For if you love those who love you, what reward will you have?" All translations seem to say that it's easy to love a friend—anyone can do that—but there's not much to be gained. At the same time, this strange commandment may cast a different light on all the Gospel teachings on love. For me, these verses are a call for real self-development—the development of a higher consciousness. These verses seem to say that it's better to love your enemy *because it's so difficult, almost impossible,* and to use doing this, doing what is so very difficult, almost impossible, in order to become a New Man or a New Woman, to be like God, "who maketh His sun to rise upon the good, and bad, and raineth upon the just and the unjust."

Christ asked his disciples to do this. Perhaps they needed to develop an ability or capacity to do this. In his book *In Search of the Miraculous*, P.D. Ouspensky quotes Gurdjieff speaking about religion, Christianity in particular, and saying, "Prolonged instruction, prolonged training is necessary to be able to turn the (other) cheek." Implying that growth or development of ability is possible with the right training, Gurdjieff goes on to say that "if this training is mechanical, it is again worth nothing because in this case it means that a man will turn his cheek because he cannot do anything else."

Gurdjieff's broad understanding of both human psychology and ancient traditional teachings left no room for the mechanical. His method required the willing participation of a student and a teacher (without a teacher, at the least, a teaching is necessary) and it requires effort, intelligence, and love from both student and teacher. For example, I heard someone say Gurdjieff told a group of people that "in four years he could teach someone to be able to turn the other cheek."

My teacher, Lord Pentland, told me that his teacher, Gurdjieff, put him to work on a project with someone he truly disliked, which resulted in the end in his not only liking this person but loving him. In fact, Pentland cautioned us that we'd lose our negativity and end up liking someone once we really worked with him or her. Of course, the key point is "really worked," and understanding what that means—and how to do it. It's one of the big living questions of the Gurdjieff Work, and an answer has never quite been formalized or written down. Hints, yes. But thankfully, no real definition. When Pentland said to me "Work is standing in a muddy field with only one galosh," he evoked a feeling that can still puzzle my mind. But my feeling understands. It informs me that to really work with someone—anyone, but especially someone you might dislike—you will feel stuck, lost, and awkward and will always want to run away. But you can decide to simply, even for a second, *stay*—be there, be present, be aware of this other human being you may not like but need to listen to. And you can *choose* to do it.

Gurdjieff was famous for keeping people around him who aroused negative feelings—other people's and probably his own. Pentland was good at this, also. From a distance of some years, I would say that not many of us really knew whether he liked us or disliked us. We did feel an objective love emanating from him, even when he was shouting at someone or looking at someone in disgust. Sometimes it seemed he was terribly demanding and almost cruel with those for whom he had the most feeling. Always though, for me, when I reported a breakthrough to understanding or found a finer moment of inner silence, he showed me his deep love.

Now both these teachers are gone, and it's more and more difficult for most of us to sort out the esoteric principles from the moral principles taught by parents and schools. So I try. When someone complains to me and asks why this person or that person is placed in this or that position, or refuses to work with this person or that person, I say, "But it's good for you; it's good for building a soul." Most people seem to like this better than being told it builds will. Both are true. Going against one's negativity, whether instinctive or justified by the rational mind, is one of the quickest ways not only to build will, but also to help create that mysterious substance known as the soul. What better way than learning to love one's enemy!

And, who is my enemy? Is it the woman who says she's a friend but speaks behind my back, or the man who belittles me but never sees me? Is it the woman who competes by subtle disparagement, or the man whose self-importance makes me feel my own inability? Or is it some part of me, such as the passive, lazy part that prevents me from walking in nature or the shy part that prevents me from sharing my talents? Just as asking who is my neighbor begins to expand my world vision, so does asking who is my enemy, and it's even more helpful to observe and feel how the answers touch me. Just writing down some examples helped me realize how damaging certain people have been and what I still feel about them. Can I learn to love them? Am I even willing to try?

For many years, two images from literature have stayed with me and have been a help: Shakespeare's quality of mercy that drops like gentle rain on "him that gives and him that takes," and James Joyce's snow falling faintly through the universe "upon all the living and the dead." Now, I understand that the realizations that came to me when hearing these lines must be deepened. The words must come down out of my head into my heart and body, where the real work can take place. I need to feel the sun shining on everyone, good and bad, and the rain falling on everyone, just and unjust. Wishing to be a child of the Father who is in heaven, I will try to love my enemy.

What Is Difficult

After I began the series of experiments that was to change my life, described in this book, my feelings were increasingly available in ways that were new—or so old that I'd almost forgotten them. Like a young child, I felt open to nature and music, to poetry and deep questions about life, and to other people in a mostly wordless way. I also felt a new kind of hope and wanted to share this with everyone I knew. It was this hope that continued to fuel further investigations and experiments.

Looking at my life, I could see areas and activities that seemed too difficult, always just out of reach. Almost every time I'd try to do something from that *too difficult* category, like playing music regularly, going for walks every day, or not losing my presence when interrupted, sooner or later I'd fail and eventually give up. Yet even with the failures, these activities, along with other difficulties, continued to attract me.

As I've written in the preface to this book, a direction came to me one early morning: *It's best to learn to love everything. Every single thing...* So, wanting to be able to love everything and also to live my own original life, I added learning to love what is difficult to my experiments—not without some hesitations and doubts. Was I setting myself up for failure and more bouts of self-criticism? Maybe, I thought, but it's worth a try.

In the first years of my experiment, several people were urging me to pick up the violin again and play in a string quartet or get together to play duos. As they urged, an old connection to playing music reappeared. Playing great music with other people had always given me great joy, but many years had passed since the time of my almost-professional career, which included study at the San Francisco Conservatory, hours of daily practice, and regular solo, orchestral, or chamber music performances. But now, finding a way to play the violin seemed very difficult—and therefore, a likely first experiment in learning to love difficulties.

I remembered my third violin teacher, Harry Hammer, who taught me so much and was so patient with my teenage eccentricities. Remarkably, he was able to practice on his violin at least five minutes a day even though he was the head of the college music department, taught several classes, and conducted regular performances of an orchestra. So, I tried practicing five minutes a day, and it was difficult. Too difficult, really. Yet, just trying gave me hope. If I could do this I might be able at least to value what is difficult.

But it was not to be. As days went by without opening my violin case and practicing the first two Kreutzer etudes I'd chosen, I felt that learning to love what is difficult might simply be *too difficult*—especially practicing at least five minutes a day.

I didn't want to give up entirely, though. Experiments in other areas of my life had convinced me that persistence was necessary, as well as study and attention. There might be other difficulties, I thought, that were *less difficult*. So, I made a list.

First on the list was the difficulty of responding with grace to interruptions, especially when I'm doing something important for myself and the time for reading or writing or pondering is so limited. Next was accepting corrections of my understanding or receiving someone else's advice. And listening to other people when it was obvious they were not listening to themselves but simply talking to convince me—and themselves—that they had great knowledge. Finally, it was very difficult to continue to speak when I knew the other person was not really listening. These four were difficult due to the demands of living with other people.

Then, there were difficulties that depended only on me. Listening to, practicing, and playing music regularly; walking outside daily; and going to bed early, at a more or less normal time, were the three most important difficulties. In a category of its own and completely dependent on my own effort, there was one more challenging difficulty—something I'd tried before and continued to wish for even when it seemed impossibly difficult—doing one thing at a time...

Gurdjieff said it. "When you do a thing, do it with the whole self, one thing at a time..." and so did the Zen Buddhists. In an old story, a student asked a Zen master, "What is Zen?" And the master answered, "Zen is doing one thing at a time."

Also, many years ago, a very wise man, Lord Pentland, once told me that the secret of inner work was to do one thing at a time, and I had tried it, not always with success. Now, remembering his words helped me once again. It is not easy to do one thing at a time in our world of multi-tasking and being overwhelmed and always too busy, but it is possible, and it is life-changing. Little by little, I was able to follow this good advice and I loved the feeling of it. Each time I chose to do only one thing, it gave me an elegant, almost extravagant feeling, like taking a little vacation from my busy life. And, it was my first entry into loving difficulties. There is much to say about this. Doing one thing at a time is like a vacation and it's also like an oasis, a clearing where I can breathe and be quiet for a moment, savoring the feeling of just what I'm doing at that moment. Clearing up the dishes has become one of the best times of my daily life! As well, trying this seems to have resulted in a new appreciation of *order*, another quality that I wanted to learn to love.

And, there was more helpful advice from Gurdjieff. "Above all," he said, "in order to do what is difficult, one must first learn to do what is easy." With this in mind, I found something so easy that it takes no time at all. In fact, it was so simple and so helpful that it appears in this book in a chapter of its own called "What Is Easy."

Little by little, many results appeared in my experiments with difficulties, almost without my trying. "Thrilled" is not a word I use very often, but in fact, I was truly thrilled the first time I was able to be more present and less reactive when interrupted. When talking with people I once found *difficult*, a new kind of listening has appeared, one that is not so concerned with what is being said or who is speaking or what they want from me. It is a more neutral listening, more all-embracing and less judgmental. And happily, though not yet playing the violin each day, I am playing the piano. The world of Bach and Schubert once more opens for me.

More and more often now, difficulties are not so difficult. There is a new feeling of relaxation in myself—more often in my body, but also in my mind and feelings. This new, broader relaxation may be the result of intending to do only one thing at a time, or trying the very easy exercise that takes no time at all, or simply trying to appreciate difficulties. It might be the result of grace, bestowed on those who set out on quixotic journeys toward apparently impossible goals. Whatever the reason, difficulties have become easier. And, I am beginning to understand—without morality entering in—something new and very important. Difficulties are necessary. Without difficulties, inner strength is seldom found and seldom called upon.

An aspect of inner strength is surely patience and my patience has grown stronger—have the interruptions helped it grow? Thankfully, this is not merely the patience of an altered attitude, only on the surface. This patience is a new *positive* feeling. More often now, it is a relaxed willingness to be present and to wait. It is not simply a surface feeling; it is a feeling in and of the whole of myself.

These experiments have made me wonder why some lives are more difficult than others and why some people have difficulties that others find easy. Is there any meaning in this? When an event comes along in my life or in someone else's life that is too painful or too difficult, like a child I sometimes want to shake my fist at heaven and say, "Stop. This is too hard!" But as I begin to be a grownup, it seems more evident that my life and its experiences are for learning. Of course, there are situations that are simply *too* difficult and truly beyond anyone's ability to bear; but very often, many difficulties can be faced and studied, and used for learning. Facing what is difficult, learning, overcoming—all this creates knowledge, understanding, and inner strength.

Difficulties can be ignored but sooner or later they will become unbearable. They can be rationalized but sooner or later they sting. And, they can be disciplined and covered over but sooner or later they emerge, unscathed, reminding us of laziness or failure or any one of the labels used by the parts of oneself too small to be called ego. Compared to some people's difficulties, mine seem fairly insignificant. I am grateful that they are demanding but not too difficult. I have been able to meet them head-on and in some instances, have learned to appreciate and love them.

Now, as I finish writing for the day and get ready to go outside for a walk, I notice a strange little habit. A very small, very insignificant part of myself has appeared to help me feel quite self-satisfied and very proud of myself for going for a walk. This little part tells me how good I am, and that doing this is enormously worthy of praise—and I haven't even gone outside! I haven't even put my coat on, and it begins to tell me what a wonderful person I am—so good, so worthy of admiration and praise, so decisive that I will be doing this walk every day from now on. What a strange, vain little thought. No wonder walking every day is difficult. It's as if I have to prove myself every time I even think of going for a walk. But now I choose not to pay much attention to this little fragment of ego. I'll simply go for a walk because I love walking outside in nature! And while I'm walking, I'll ponder a little about what I've learned.

This experiment is far from finished, but now I know several simple things about what is difficult and what is not. Now, I can experience many levels of love whether I am playing music or listening to another person, going to bed at a decent hour or doing one thing at a time—I can love seeing why something is difficult and feeling the energy that results from facing it directly, which often gives me the taste of joy that unifies. Most of all, I love knowing old difficulties and attitudes can change into what is new, and possible.

What Is Easy

I sit at my desk in Colorado and my attention is drawn outside to a sudden summer storm. Not unusual in the mountains, in the afternoon. Somehow, the lightning and thunder and heavy rain outside help me to be here, inside my office, trying to ponder. How to approach the many aspects of my life that simply seem too difficult to love? How to love difficulties?

"And above all, in order to do what is difficult, one must first learn to do what is easy," Gurdjieff said. When I read this for the first time, it stopped me, and now it makes me pause again. I have been trying to learn to love difficulties with mixed results, and here is something else to ponder. I wonder what this means. Experience has taught me, or so it seems, that almost nothing is easy. And in trying to understand Gurdjieff's advice, I'm not quite sure what "difficult" means and even less certain about what is "easy."

I can recall a few memories of moments of joy accompanied by a wonderful ease of action, but all these moments seem to be out of reach now. And all of those joyful moments were completely dependent on outside circumstances—a moment of brilliant light coming through the lilacs over my head, hearing as if for the first time remarkable music, the right note of approval in a teacher's voice, an impromptu dinner with my family. Recalling these moments, I wonder what is possible now. Can I initiate such moments, from *myself*? But yes, the whole enterprise I am engaged in and have recorded on these pages was based on this very possibility—that I wouldn't depend entirely on accidental circumstances, that something could originate in and from me, that I could in fact learn to love something that is very difficult to do.

Surely Gurdjieff's suggestion would be a first step in learning to love difficulties. It means finding an action that would be so easy that even I could try it, and by trying to do it with intention, learn its meaning; and by learning what it means, learn to love it.

While searching my experience and the information I've collected over the years, the first thing that comes to mind is an exercise for stretching the attention—and the intention—that was given to me many years ago. Now I see it more clearly as a simple but powerful exercise. In fact, when I try it now or give it to someone else, I call it the exercise that takes no time or the exercise for busy people. Those of us who have too much to do every day can use this exercise because it takes no time. All that is required is remembering to do it, and remembering why. Of course, each time one tries an exercise, whether spiritual or physical, it's very important to know *why*. Here it is:

First, ask yourself, "Which shoe do I put on first? The right or the left?" Then, put on the *other* shoe. While putting on the other shoe, silently repeat the following words: "I wish to be able to struggle with myself." If you forget and it's not too late, immediately start over.

If ordinarily the right shoe goes on first, put the left shoe on or vice versa. Choose the *other*, the non-habitual, each and every time. Practicing this exercise will increase the awareness of the sense, the sensation, of your body, especially the feet. Also, there may be increased awareness of the *why* of the exercise—the reason to do it. Then, other words silently repeated when putting on the other shoe may be preferred. For instance, "I wish to be myself." or "I wish to be."

And this exercise can expand. After practicing with shoes for a while, trying with stockings or socks also can be helpful. Again, it's about discovering which one usually goes first—and then putting on the other, non-habitual stocking first.

And what about other clothing? Getting ready for bed or dressing for the day, putting on a jacket, coat, sweater, shirt, slacks or pants, pajamas or robe can be opportunities for affirming both an intention and a wish.

But the body begins to learn new ways and tries to do things differently. After doing this exercise for many weeks, there is less clarity about which foot or arm would go first. Then, it becomes even more important to find the sensation of the feet and notice which foot seems *less* ready to go into its shoe, and choose that less-ready foot to go first. And each time, trying not to forget that underneath the sensing and choosing, I need to remind myself *why* I am doing this— remembering the wish to be able to struggle with myself, remembering that I want to be able to say no to the laziness and unwillingness that support a passive life.

Of course, this exercise shows me that, like everything else, beginning something is relatively easy—but as it's practiced over time, it becomes less easy. After a while, I have to work to remember to try, or after remembering, to agree with myself to try. Boredom has appeared, and an excuse for not trying because I am "too tired" has appeared more than once. This is strange and quite silly. How could I be too tired to do something added on very lightly, almost invisibly, to an action that I need to do and will do, tired or not? This must be what illusion is all about—the world of illusion must be built on similar excuses. It's easy in this world to find excuses not to be active, but this is not the "what is easy" I wish to do. However, directly seeing this strange excuse of being too tired has given me additional energy for wanting to try, which is a bonus.

This exercise, repeated again and again, is probably the simplest act I can find right now, and small moments of progress have appeared. I've tried to do this in the morning, during the day, or before going to bed, while remembering what I want and looking for the actual sensation of my limbs. Maybe I'll build a reserve of patience and determination while getting to know my feet and legs better. Patience and determination—good allies in learning to love both what is difficult and what is easy.

Now, results appear, and I begin to understand that doing something simple and easy, intentionally and consistently, can create a new ability. When trying something difficult now, it is not so difficult. It's as if an entirely new ability is there, not always, but from time to time. Perhaps a new energy has accumulated in me. Feeling more able, I see that this new energy may support the ability needed to face what is difficult—or any other as-yet-unnamed aspect of my life.

I wish to be able, not only to face the difficulties and do what is difficult, I wish to be able to *love* what is difficult—just as I wish to be able to love all the other aspects of my life and all the parts of the amazing world around me. And, all of this—wishing, being able, loving—becomes true for me just now as I write.

Looking out the window above and beyond my desk, the sky is lighter now than it was when I began to ponder and write about what is easy. There are individual clouds and they are in motion, revealing larger areas of blue sky; the leaves of the big tree still tremble and glisten with raindrops, but the lightning and thunder have stopped. The midday storm has moved on to the east.

Seeing more now, and more quietly, I understand once again that in every moment in which this simple, direct seeing is possible, every last particle of my inner world and every last particle of the outer world seems to overflow with life and silence and beauty. And now I feel ready for life and the moment when my arm will to go into my sweater, and I get to choose.

Not Knowing

In April 2011, my journal entry was about a mysterious part of my inner world that I had just experienced, not for the first time, but more or less intentionally. This part was what I came to call the One Who Does Not Know.

We were staying at an old farmhouse near Philadelphia with twenty-five other people, and each morning we'd sit quietly together to begin the day. One morning, as I sat in front of the others, trying to speak a few words, I felt a strong need to return again and again to just watching and to finding something in my inner world that does not know, does not describe or tell me what to try, and does not even want to know. I was determined, and wanted to make something like an effortless effort to sit very quietly and to simply watch. I suggested to the others that we could try this together. Body relaxed, mind simply watching, returning again and again to just sitting.

Thankfully, and surely as the result of grace, after a time of working this way, the knowing—so full of information and techniques—stopped. It stopped telling me what to try or how to do it, stopped commenting or worrying about what someone else might think, it simply stopped whispering its advice to me. Stillness appeared in the room. My body became deeply relaxed even as my mind became deeply quiet. I was present, and free. Rather than seeing *from* the body/mind, I was looking *toward* it. My whole organism had become a *fact*, a wonderful living miraculous *fact*. After we got up I could see the others must have had similar experiences. Every one of us looked happy, relaxed, and very much younger.

An experience like this doesn't happen often. It can never be forced. But it helps to remember that it's possible. It is a gift, a result of grace, and at the same time it's the result of a necessary struggle—the effortless effort—to be free of the domination of information, knowing what to do, wanting to be always right, and the seductive power of the educated mind. This is a struggle that can be carried out in life, which gives us many opportunities, and it also a very important part of the struggle to sit quietly. Of course, it helps to sit with others who are also struggling.

Later on, I was sorry not to be able to come to such freedom again. But, the years bring a little wisdom, thankfully, and I've decided not to be too greedy. Now, I understand that even one or two experiences of real, complete inner freedom may be enough for a whole lifetime. Certainly those experiences gave me material to work with for many years, years of remembering and pondering and searching for not-knowing. In their own way, they have given me both a deepening of my wish to *be* and something similar to the original experience. As I remember that experience now some years later, I can still taste the freedom of it, and the happiness that comes from being just who and where I am, doing just what I am supposed to be doing.

There is one part of myself who does not know. It's alive in me, and I am grateful. But sometimes I wonder how it stays alive, living as it does under the weight of a great amount of that which is known—useless information mostly, deposited over the years. And sadly, too often the bits and pieces of this heavy weight of information prevent real silence. When I want to be very quiet inside my mind and body, the one in me who knows too much is quick to tell me how to proceed and what methods and steps to take. It's also quick to comment and tell me I'm right, or wrong. It goes out of its way to give me suggestions on everything, especially inner work, gathered from books, magazines or online articles, and overheard wisdom, using many, many words.

The part of me that does not know isn't always evident. It's a mystery because it has no defined borders or form. Being the one who does not know, it's also the one who does not do. It performs almost no actions except to support my seeing the truth. Although it seldom speaks in words, in rare moments it has spoken and in those moments has communicated great knowledge to me. Is there such a one in me now? I say *Yes,* and feel the challenge to find it now, within the density of the world of written words. In spite of all the words and thoughts, I know it must be there.

Some years ago, my dear Parisian friend told me to know what I know. Remembering the sound of her voice, a *koan* comes to me now: *How do you know what you know and what you don't know?*

A journal note turned up recently, in the way that interesting things have been turning up as I write about learning to love. Written many years ago in San Francisco, it describes a moment of living more freely and also something about not knowing, or so it seems to me now in retrospect:

> A moment today while sitting in front of the upright loom, ready to begin a new tapestry. Design pinned to the side of the loom; skeins of wool in colors for the design all laid out; warp threads twangy and beautiful in their white emptiness, almost singing with right tension, waiting for the weaver to put the weft in place. Ready to begin. What a wonderful moment this is, everything waiting in the moment of beginning, not knowing anything except what is there. Wishing, hoping, planning that all these materials will come together to make a weaving. I love this moment. Not doing anything. Simply ready to begin.

As a young girl I felt the simplicity of being simply ready to begin, *not knowing* yet looking forward to the joy of discovery. I remember myself then, reading and studying, trying to understand and figure things out, looking at what it might mean to be a grown-up. Making pottery and firing it using sand and the summer heat. Designing a folding chair. Secretly entering art contests, and winning. Studying the way a pedal going up and down makes a wheel turn round and round. Climbing up a tree to a meeting point of branches where I could sit above our house and yard to be alone and think—and attempt the composition of a tone poem inspired by the Grand Canyon suite. Digging a real World War II fox hole and sitting in it to feel what soldiers fighting overseas must feel. And much more. Crazy things. Sensible things. Very private things.

In the beginning, living this way wasn't forced. It simply felt like me—and who I was and what I wanted. But gradually other motives crept in. Showing off to others, getting good grades in school, feeling grown-up and important, being able to give the right answer to questions the teacher asked, and much more, too—those motives were never the same as my original wish to understand. And not knowing the right answers began to make me uneasy.

My original wish was about life and learning how to live and be myself, and even about learning to love, although I could never have put any of this into words. When I experienced the part of myself that doesn't know, it felt like the center of happiness—happiness to be only who and where I am. Not knowing meant being open to feel the joy of life itself and also to perceive its mystery, to explore, to be curious, to respond or not, and to live with questions that opened up again and again to a new land of new experiences. It is still true. For this part of me, life itself is still most important, whether I am exploring or resting. And because no one can tell me where that new land is, or how to get there—or how to live in it—I understand how important it is to find the one in me who does not know. The other parts pride themselves in what they know but they can't lead me. The truth is, they don't know, but fool themselves and others by acting the part of someone who has knowledge. I have been too adept at acting this part.

One day last year as we returned from a midday concert I felt the heavy presence of the one who knows—the showoff, the scholar, the determinedly superior being, the someone who has knowledge—and it was finally enough. I had just finished explaining some esoteric bit of musical knowledge when I saw that my long cultivation of that one who knows might be nearing its end.

"I am *so* tired of knowing everything," I announced. The others in the car laughed. They had already noticed that I was a know-it-all, I'm sure, and found me really tiresome at times, but had accepted me in spite of this. I laughed along with them at hearing myself make such an outrageous statement. But inside, I knew this was a moment of truth— one big crack in something strongly built as defense against the outside world. There were already cracks in the walls, results of moments such as this, or the one in front of the loom, or coming to the direct experience of not knowing while a group of us sat together. Moments like these have slowly rearranged my inner world.

Now, my participation in an outer life that revolves around searching and finding is not as active as when I was a younger—I no longer weave or design tapestries, my foxhole digging days have passed—but there is still much to explore. I continue to study and collect data and information about many things, such as ancient history, a particular idea or conversation found in a book or shared by a friend, or a new piece of music and the inspiration behind it. What's important now are areas that touch both my inner and outer worlds. Rearranging the plants in the garden or on the deck, experimenting with new recipes, writing about my experiences and once in a while writing down a poem that's appeared in my mind, creating a beautiful, orderly living space—these are all favorite activities. Along with many good conversations and reading lots of books!

But when any of this feels like drudgery and no longer brings the joy, excitement, and the heightened awareness of discovery—the manifestations of the energy of love—I know that something in me has fallen into the old habits, the attitudes of a sleeping person who dreams of knowing everything and has forgotten what freedom feels like. Remembering the taste of that freedom, once again I feel the presence of the One Who Does Not Know, patiently waiting for me to see all this. And, I am grateful.

A Prayer

Everyone I meet seems to know something—usually a lot! Everyone I talk to sooner or later seems to know more than I do, or thinks they do, and they are quick to show me that this is so.

Is there no one who is content to simply listen as I speak? It's a real difficulty for me, this feeling of not being listened to. I want to find a way to live with that and it's been added to my list of the difficulties I want to love.

There is another difficulty I'd like to try to understand and eventually love—as often as I can remember. I would like simply to listen and let others tell me what is right or wrong from their own store of information—everyone seems to have one. Even if I fail too many times in trying to accept being told what is right or wrong, I can learn to relax and simply try to listen. After all, I am trying to learn how to love and in particular, trying to love *not knowing*. While writing this, a note of caution comes up in me and it has formed a little prayer.

Please, I ask, do not let me think I know more or better than anyone else. Help me try to simply listen to another person speaking. Please let me really listen to this other person—not so much to the words or the tone, but to something behind the sound and meaning of the words. Let me try to listen to the one who doesn't know in this person—it's there behind the words that are meant to inform me and set me on the right course. Then there could be two of us—two human beings who do not know. For a moment we might be simply present together, speaking, listening, not knowing.

Not Too Busy

Again in April, 2011, as I wrote in my journal, I experienced another part of my inner world: The One Who Is Not Busy. This was a close companion of another part, The One Who Does Not Know. My experience with that One appears in another chapter, Not Knowing, in this book.

My friend Darlene Cohen had died in January of 2011. Her death was a huge loss for many people—friends and students, along with members of the San Francisco Zen Center and the Buddhist community in the San Francisco Bay Area and beyond. Mourning her death, I bought one of her books called *The One Who Is Not Busy*. The title comes from a short Zen story. A teacher approaches another teacher who is sweeping some stone steps and scolds him, implying that he is too busy. The other teacher, standing quietly while holding his broom, responds by saying, "You should know there is one who is not busy."

I pondered this story for several months and came to see its resemblance to Gurdjieff's idea that human beings consist of many I's, each of which claim for a moment to be the only one. When I read the idea of many I's for the first time, it touched me deeply. While moving from childhood into adulthood I had puzzled—and suffered—over the shifts in my outer personality. They seemed completely automatic—simply responses, reactions, to outer circumstances, such as different subjects taught in high school classes and the teachers in front of those classes. I was one way with my family and another with friends. I was different with each of the boys I dated. Even on first reading, I knew the idea of many I's was true and welcomed its corollary idea—the possible development of real individuality, *unfragmented individuality*, capable of responding voluntarily to life in all its variety of energies and manifestations.

The Zen story provided a good example of this idea of many I's: even though someone might appear to be very busy, there could be an inner part—another "I"—who is not busy and is free to meditate. This would be The One Who Is Not Busy. After experimenting a little, I saw this for myself. There *is* one there in my inner world who is not at all busy; in fact, this one is completely relaxed, waiting, and simply observing. I can't help but be a little in awe of this one!

Now I can understand Thomas Merton's statement that that allowing oneself "to surrender to too many demands, to commit oneself to too many projects, to want to help everyone in everything, is to succumb to the violence of our times." Along with that understanding, I felt a strong dislike of that part of me who fancied that she knew everything and therefore felt fully equipped to help others. Yet, at the same time she seemed burdened by too much to do, too many people to write or call—exhausted by this violence. The avidity with which I tackled life was too often exhausting, for me and for those who lived with me.

Could I learn to live with that greedy part? In trying to look more closely, I noticed that something was missing. It was very natural for me to do many, many things, to have concerns and demands and projects, and very natural to wish to help others. But the mind was missing. My body was strong; it had been a source of pride for me since the days of batting a ball as well as the boys, catching a football equally well, riding a boy's bike, or climbing the highest trees. My feelings were also strong. Being able to feel what needed to be done—especially in order to help others—had become a way of life for me. It felt right to be concerned and dedicated to helping others while trying to meet the demands of my own life. But, was there any intelligence in all this? I could not expect that young girl who loved to read and loved to play baseball to think about this too carefully. She was young. That excuse is not valid now. Now, I need an attentive mind. Joined with a body, which is no longer young, though still somewhat proud of its abilities, and feelings that have been honed by life and are more attuned to the good, real attention could become real intelligence. And, intelligence could and does create wholeness—a whole person.

Recently, I mentioned having a very long to-do list, and a friend asked me what I'd do if I weren't too busy and the possessor of a very long to-do list. He was trying to trick me, so he added, "Probably you'd find other items for that list. And then you'd be too busy again!"

In that moment, I saw a different way to be busy. This way was about needing and wanting and trying to do what I really wanted and liked—what I really loved. Yes, there were many I's, and each had its requirements, but surely some of those parts of myself were more essential than others. Surely there were I's alive since childhood, almost forgotten but still close to who I was meant to be. So I answered this friend who challenged me about being busy. "If I weren't too busy, I would play the violin, practice several hours a day, and best of all, play chamber music. I would paint watercolors again. I would walk every day, enjoying Great Nature, and rest when I needed to rest."

I could see it. My whole life would be about doing many things and would be very busy, but it would be busyness without violence and feeling forced and overwhelmed. My whole life would be about doing things that I love and, following what I've discovered in writing this book, learning to love more and more parts of my life—even the concerns and issues and projects dictated to me by life itself.

Many years ago, Lord Pentland gave me a task to do something I liked once a day. It was an impossible task. Every day I had to face the fact of not knowing what I liked and therefore not being able to do it. Finally, after many days of failure, a moment of awareness appeared. I had more or less given up trying the task and was reading late one night. The house was very quiet. A bedside light illuminated the pages of my book. I was alone. Without trying anything at all, I realized the truth: I liked being there. He seemed very pleased when I reported this and said something that was quite mysterious. "Yes," he said, "it's all about sincerity, and sincerity means to *see*."

Now, remembering his words, I also remember that in the innermost region of my innermost world there is One Who Is Not Busy. I feel the truth of this. This One is completely relaxed, patient and quiet, simply watching over me and the world around me, and together with The One Who Does Not Know, serving something even more patient, even more quiet, even higher. Serving the unfragmented individuality that is a representative of the Source, and not just another "I."

Disappointment

In the early days of excitement and happiness after moving to a new life—to a new city and a new country—I believed that disappointment would never be able to pull me down again. In the beginning of my new life in Toronto, there seemed to be time for many activities I had missed in San Francisco. Just walking was exciting. Living once again with changing seasons was exciting. Exploring was exciting. And very close by, there was a beautiful old area to explore. Only a few blocks north of my husband's condo, it was a beautiful area in which to walk. There were streets with tall old trees and stately old houses that contrasted sharply with my husband's modern condo eleven floors above a noisy downtown street. Even in winter, when the trees had lost their leaves or deep snow covered the yards of the old houses, I loved those walks.

In the early days, I walked every day, taking in the beauty and grandeur of the old houses, studying the brickwork patterns, counting the pillars, towers, and fireplace chimneys, noticing the style of windows, and admiring the spacious yards with trees and plants that changed colors each season. I tried to catch glimpses through the windows of the artwork or chandeliers inside the front rooms of the houses so I could imagine the beautiful interiors. There were large houses with many rooms, and smaller houses, duplexes, discrete apartment buildings, and town houses—all placed within a gracious natural setting. Rain, snow—the seasons never diminished the quality of this neighborhood.

At the same time, lovely images and feelings of what it would be like to live in such houses began to fill my head and heart during my walks. Day after day, the pleasure of daydreams added to the pleasure of walking in nature in this beautiful neighborhood. These were just the kind of houses I'd always dreamed of, and now I dreamed about a future of real possibilities, which might just come true.

Months passed. Eventually, several years had gone by since I moved to Toronto, and there was less joy in my walks. I began to realize that a life in this neighborhood was not for me—that I would never live in a big old house under trees surrounded by gardens. I began to notice that much of my love for these old houses with their windows and fireplaces and gardens was more about a longing to possess. A part of me believed that some of this would be—could be—mine. Yet seeing this, I began to know that this was not to be. And I began to feel disappointed. In fact, my disappointment was so great that some days I couldn't bring myself to enter this neighborhood. I was actually in pain, suffering from a deep feeling of disappointment that seemed to fill all the spaces in my body. I felt paralyzed. Stopped by disappointment, there were fewer and fewer walks. Staying inside was easier than facing that feeling whenever I saw the old houses and quiet streets.

Disappointment can be severe. When I see disappointment and its results in me or in others, I think of Hans Christian Andersen's "The Little Match Girl." Disappointment seems to create something inside me that feels like a hungry child outside in the cold, looking into a warm room where people are talking, laughing, and eating together, while she is outside in the snow, starving and about to freeze to death. Reading the story, one feels sorry for that child. When her story appears within one's inner world, it's easy to feel self-pity—and self-judgment reinforces this. For me, both self-pity and self-judgment are both very much part of disappointment. *You'll never be happy again*, the inner critic tells me. *How could you fall for that? How could you be so stupid?*

With luck, however, and what is called resilience, most of us recover from disappointment. In my experience, however, recovery is usually accompanied by and dependent on the arising of a new hope. And with hope, the circle begins again—possibilities appear and disappear, hope is renewed and fades, disappointment overwhelms—again and again. Life seems to keep many of us human beings in just such a circle, beginning with hope and creating expectations, leading to disappointment.

Give up all expectation, we are told. I had said this to other people and to myself. I had tried, sometimes with some success, to let go of expectations, until another hope-filled event came along that was irresistible—a new job, a new way of thinking, a new home, new friends, or especially a new lover. Until sooner or later, following the natural course of things in my inner world, expectations were not met, and disappointment appeared.

But a few years earlier, I had taken up a cause. I was on a Way. *I wanted to learn to love.* So once again, cautiously, the walks began. But these walks were for a different kind of seeing than those early walks when I was enchanted by spaciousness, beauty, and antiquity, and the possibility of living in one of these houses was still alive. Trying to see more clearly the houses as they stood breathing under the weight of their years, it was easier to avoid the wish to possess them. The pangs of disappointment were there, but I tried to look beneath and around the disappointment and the possessiveness, simply to see the houses.

Once again, I noticed patterns of brickwork but now a feeling for the craftsmanship of the brickwork came to me, and with it, a feeling for long-dead craftsmen who so patiently and artistically created these patterns. Often, there were walls and decorative trims on walls, border patterns around doors and windows—ornate yet simple, almost always mathematical in basis, almost never random in the modern style, these patterns had meaning. They spoke of a time when meaning was important, not something to be avoided in the search for the next new thing.

I watched as many windows were replaced. Thankfully, in this Toronto neighborhood some of the mullioned panes remained but many of the old curved or beveled beauties were exchanged for modern double-panes.

Most of the old trees were left in place, and not too many new ones were planted. The same perennials bloomed year after year. I put some of the same plants into pots in my deck garden, with little success. The deck faced north and perennials need deep roots. Finally, I let them be. Passing by the plants that thrived in the old neighborhood, I simply looked and admired and walked on.

Once, I watched the roof of a corner tower being covered with copper. The workmen were young yet their work was careful and faithful to the style of this old home, probably built in the 19th century. They seemed to respect the house and their own work. We exchanged a few smiles from day to day, and after they finished I continued to admire the glow of the copper facing, watching it fade and weather until it matched the colors of the rest of the house.

Several years later, I was able to enjoy my walks again. Simply looking, admiring and feeling a kinship with the craftsmen who built these old places while at the same time, feeling the scale of the living that had gone on in these houses—the servants who worked so many hours of the day caring for all those rooms upstairs and downstairs, building fires, cleaning fireplaces, cooking with wood- or coal-burning stoves, serving, mending. I felt a little sad when I saw the renovation signs and knew the interior was being gutted, but I said hello to members of the young families who, in the fashion of wealthy young people these days in Toronto, were able to buy an ancient house, renovate the interior, put up basketball nets and play equipment in the yard, hire a garden design firm, and park at least one expensive car in the driveway. I admired their taste and their obvious belief and hope in their own futures.

Little by little, the neighborhood and its life became more real to me as I gave it more attention, and a shift took place in me, a shift away from my own hopes and dreams to a sense and feeling of and for the outside world.

More often then, there were magical moments when the world simply appeared, in all its color and shape and variety while I was simply there—only a part of it. My point of view was shifting. I was less interested in feeling deprived of living a life in this beautiful old neighborhood, which had changed me into a kind of hungry child—always outside, wanting into the feast. And, I was less and less interested in always *wanting* and always being disappointed. As I received a more realistic view of the houses and yards and trees, the daydreams faded.

Just walking through that neighborhood close to our busy downtown street became a help. The silence under the old trees, the sounds of the birds in their branches, and the stately presence of the old houses helped me. As the daydreams faded, so did any pleasure I might take from them. In their place there was something new.

In whatever strange and unconscious ways my individuality had been formed, no allowance had been made in me to know truly what I want. Stumbling along, trying to live the best way possible, following the lead of those around me, I had learned to want to possess and own things—houses, clothes, status, beauty, love, relationship, wisdom—an endless list. No wonder trying to have all these things had led to disappointment. I had seldom learned what it is that I myself want. Now, after all the walks through this beautiful old neighborhood, I felt closer to that. Instead of always wanting to possess, I felt a new appreciation for simply knowing what I want, and a new feeling for the truth of who I am.

Now, I have experienced what disappointment can teach me, which is not about possessing or owning. When I can find the determination and strength not to be defeated but to go on trying to see more, to be even more attentive, disappointment can show me *what I want*. That's all. And that is precious. It doesn't matter whether I will ever have it. Maybe it is for the future, maybe it was somewhere in the past and therefore familiar. If only for a moment, to simply know what it is that I want is an extraordinary experience. It provides the richest, warmest, most wonderful meal any little girl might have.

Truth

For me, to love the truth would mean living it, voluntarily, not out of fear or moral judgment, not because I was forced into such a life, but choosing truth. Choosing my truth. Choosing what I know is true.

How do I know what is true? I need to be very careful here, and as sincere as possible. First, I need to know what I know, which is what I've learned and verified by my own experience. And, if I haven't learned this well enough, I need to experiment, repeat, and continue trying to verify. Otherwise, when the time comes to make decisions, I will still not know what to do.

This book is one of my experiments. Many parts of it are an attempt to look at myself from the viewpoint of the world of instinct, sensation, and feeling—those hidden currents that run deep in everyone's life. Mostly unseen, too often they undermine the rational, logical decisions that seem so simple and apt yet don't seem to have much lasting power. And, it is the knowledge obtained by the instinct, sensation, and feeling that the mind needs—that I need—in order to become unified, a whole intelligent person capable of understanding. In trying to look directly at my experiences, and writing down my thoughts and feelings as they respond to these experiences, I am attempting to bring them back to life. For me, and possibly for a reader who finds his or her own experiences enlivened by mine, I believe this can truly be the *Way of*

Experience, a way toward being in front of the truth of life itself, and then and there, glimpsing the great Truth all the great religious traditions speak of, the Source.

At the same time, in asking what is true for me in this life, I am faced with another question. Can I live my truth? In addition to knowing what is true, what is required in order to live it? What force or will is needed to be able to choose when there is clearly a choice to be made?

"I came to tell you that if it rains, the streets get wet," Gurdjieff said when asked what his teaching was about. I say, "If you stay up too late, you are tired the next morning." Two simple *facts*. The second could be one of the many facts that show up in looking at almost anyone's life. If I drink too much coffee, I can't get to sleep. If I wait too long to sign up for a class, I won't get in. If I treat another person badly, the relation between us becomes threatened. And so on. Everyone, even me, has long lists of those simple truths. I know they are true, but how often do I choose to obey their truth? Gurdjieff's statement is so simple that its meaning could be easily missed. It's so true that immediately, with even a little pondering, I know that it comes from a level of wisdom that mostly eludes me—because it is so simple and true. Even in my usual state I know better than to go out in the rain expecting to keep dry without an umbrella. Preferring to remain dry, I carry an umbrella or stay inside until the rain stops. That is a *fact*.

So—*if I stay up too late, I am tired the next morning*. Why doesn't that equally simple statement lead to a simple action—why don't I go to bed earlier? Do I like being too tired or sleeping too late the next morning? Not really. What's going on? What's at stake here? Energy, yes, but is there something else?

In beginning to write this chapter about truth, I used the word *voluntarily*. That may be the clue to what's at stake. What is missing too often in my life—a life in which I do in fact wish to live my truth—is the ability to *do* this. But that is the whole point of loving the truth. I wish to be able to know what is true without fear and also to choose it in freedom, from myself, out of love. I wish to come to a moment when, in front of truth, I am stopped, and can be still for a moment. And, now, coming to the truth that I wish for, and writing it down and then rereading it, a little feeling stirs in me as if it is waking up. Once again I remember that the hidden parts are needed—the instinct, the sensation, and perhaps most of all, the feeling of what is here just now. Without their participation no seemingly wise decisions will triumph in either my inner or outer life, and no amount of my own wise analysis or advice from others will provide the inner force needed to truly love—and live—the truth.

Order

During my first visit to Paris, I was part of a group of men and women who met one evening to share thoughts, feelings, and impressions about our efforts to wake up. Some of the meeting was in French, some was in English; all of it was intense. Sincerity was demanded by the circumstances. When we were asked whether we felt our inner work toward presence was fraudulent, I felt required to speak as truly as possible and others surely felt the same. By the end of the meeting, a new energy, deeply silent and profoundly alive, filled the room and each of us sitting there.

Later, we met with a larger group of people. We were all ages and more than one nationality, sitting together without words and trying to be relaxed. A man sat quietly in front of us. Sometimes he was silent; sometimes, speaking softly, he directed our attention to what was possible at that moment. What he said might have been in French; it might have been in English. For me, it didn't matter. I heard directly, without a need for interpretation. Almost at the end, he said, "Consciousness comes down into the body and puts everything into order." And something happened in me, in my own body. There it was: the experience of real order, appearing in me. I watched as an inner process began, and as it continued, my inner world was put into order. My mind, my heart, and my body—each took its place under the light of something higher, the source of life itself. Then, he spoke of obedience. Were his words spoken aloud or whispered in my heart and mind? I remember only that these words came to me: *Order means to obey*.

From that evening until the present time, my wish for order—truly, a wish to love order—was fueled by the memory of the events of that evening in Paris and also by an old question: *What do I obey?* Lord Pentland had given us this question in San Francisco during a meeting many years before I went to Paris. It has blended with a wish for order—and both the feeling of my inability and my ability to obey—to become a larger, more inclusive question. It has become a fundament for my study of myself. At any moment: *What do I obey?*

Quite a few years have passed since both those meetings took place. Now, it seems most important to realize that I've been given many precious gifts. Each of these simple statements was a unique gift. I have tried to love order by learning to listen and to obey those gifts.

Years later, a new ability was given to me, quietly, almost unnoticeably, in much the way as those few words were entrusted to us in a meeting in San Francisco and were so simply given in Paris.

This occurred during a week when I was alone in Toronto. It was a rare opportunity that summer to be alone for eight days, and I had a wonderful time. It was a surprise to see my own daily order appearing after only a few days. Times to eat, to sleep, to read, or write all seemed true to something besides having to go to a job or needing to fix a meal for a partner. This was my time. In only a few days a kind of rhythm—I called it appropriateness—appeared, and I welcomed the relaxation it brought. Now, several years later, I don't recall exactly when this special gift first appeared. I only know it came to me that week, and it has continued to help me ever since.

Without quite knowing which day it began or where it came from, I began to be aware in quite a simple way of having an object in my hand, of knowing that this object belonged in a specific place, and then, of the need to simply put it there. A simple act of obedience. Without planning it, I stopped putting something down to be done later and began to simply and finally put it where it belonged. And miraculously, this simple action has continued, more or less, to the present time.

A very simple gift, isn't it? But it has had many benefits. First of all it seems to give me more time. In another chapter, I wrote about a feeling of a vacation or an oasis when doing only one thing at a time. Simply putting things away in their right place with no stops along the way has given me the same delicious feeling. It is a simple awareness of an object in my hand and the fact that it belongs in its place. And it seems to take less time to do this than to return to an object abandoned and waiting to be put away *later*. I find myself wishing to listen to this awareness and give it my attention, and then to put the object away quietly, and without too much hesitation. I begin to understand obedience.

At the same time, this gift has helped me not to worry so much. I want to remember the fact of the gifts I have been given and not waste my time worrying about how many gifts I missed by not being open and relaxed—and worrying about whether or not the gifts were deserved. By simply obeying the call toward order, trying to listen and to love, I return the gifts to where they come from, again and again—so they may be given, again and again.

The Idea of Death

Over the last few years, I have tried to learn how to love many parts of myself and my life, and trying this has given me new impressions, new understanding, and new strength. But underneath, and surrounding all this material of my life there is something that needs to be recognized. It feels like a demand just now. There is something living on the other side of life itself. I know it's time to look more closely at the idea of death, even begin to have a feeling about it. Could I love it simply as an idea, as well as an experience of the loss of another living thing or as the inevitable conclusion of my own life? The time has come to look directly at the idea of death.

Feeling what's at stake helps. My own death is inevitable, and everything and everyone in my life will also die sooner or later. Coming to some kind of understanding of these *facts* would surely help me not only to be somewhat free of fear and anxiety. This understanding might help me learn to love everything and everyone *more*, even myself.

Tibetan practices emphasize the need for a clear, strong mind at the moment the spirit departs from the body. The practice of self-observation and self-remembering in the Gurdjieff work may be a preparation for this.

Breathing in, Breathing Out

Death is in the air this morning. My friend Dagmar died last Wednesday and the actor, Philip Seymour Hoffman, died yesterday. She was 68; he was 48. And just now, two dear friends are facing death in California. So here I am, trying to take the idea of death into my mind and feeling—the fact of it, yes, but also its meaning. On one side, it hurts to no longer have the person in my life, or in the life of the world or the culture, as Hoffman was. There's another loss to the world that also cut deeply. The poet Seamus Heaney died last August leaving only his words and our admiration. It saddens me to know these people are no longer here.

On the other side of loss, there's a different view. I see a movement of energy at every moment coming down, bringing life to this earth and its film of organic life—coming down. And, at the same time, there is another movement constantly ascending, taking life away from our earth, returning it to its source. An enormous exchange.

On my own much smaller scale, I am sometimes aware of an exchange taking place within and around me. The awareness of the process of breathing seems to be as close as I can come to understanding an exchange of substances, a process of transformation. I watch my breath coming in and going out, bringing my body nutrition and giving back substances that help transform the air. As I follow the process, an understanding forms itself, an understanding of the great transformations that constantly, in every moment, create—and destroy—our world. Breathing in, breathing out—birth and death, the two great forces.

As I write my thoughts just now, and feel the loss of my friend, I also feel sadness, and awareness, and a kind of acceptance. There is a new relaxation down deep in my body. I look out the window and see the pale blue sky with low clouds lit by the sun, the snow in patterned patches on the deck where the statue of the Buddha sits, his face a picture of inner silence, unmoved by human comings and goings. In the light from the window, I see the plants on the shelf next to the table, with leaves that tremble slightly from the warm air coming out of the ceiling vent. I try to come back to thinking about and *feeling* my question. Can I learn to love the idea of death?

I feel myself here, and in the midst of this awareness of life and beauty, I'm remembering with distaste the echo of my brusque words to my husband when he interrupted me this morning.

Here I am, between sorrow and the inexorable, *essential* process of transformation, accepting them both and accepting to be here, if only for a moment in time, in this place, on this earth, knowing that there is something very much larger than any of us that breathes us in and out.

Freedom

Many years ago, in 1984, I was living in Marin County north of San Francisco. It was there that I received another view of death. On February 13, I arrived home late after working all day in Oakland and attending several meetings in San Francisco that evening. I had driven from Oakland across the Bay Bridge to San Francisco for the meetings and then across the Golden Gate Bridge to Larkspur. Tired, too tired to be sociable, I watched television for a short while and then went to bed, alone in the spare bedroom.

The next morning, February 14, I was awakened early by an incredible feeling of happiness, of pure joy. I lay in bed, very relaxed, experiencing that joy for what seemed like a long time. Then the phone rang.

I got up, went out to the kitchen, and answered it. A friend was calling to tell me that Lord Pentland had died that morning.

In the days that followed, of course I was shocked, and each day I deeply mourned the loss of him. But at the same time, the taste of the joy I'd felt was present. It was such a *complete* joy—free of any cause or content—and it came to me that this was the feeling of perfect freedom. Each time I remembered the taste of it, I felt joy and happiness. He had shared that with me. Maybe there were others who felt his passing in the same way. I don't know. I know what I experienced. That experience set a standard for me that would always in this lifetime be one of my highest measures of consciousness, awareness, and freedom.

One of my daughters told me she felt this same joy at a distance, when her grandmother, my mother, died. I did not. I was there with her during the whole process of transition and was transformed by her courage and presence and by the immense power of an experience of pure truth. The words of the Divine Liturgy of Saint John Chrysostom came back to me then. "Christ, our God, You were crucified but *conquered death* by death." As a witness to my mother's passing into another world, I stood and said aloud, "*She has conquered death with death.*"

Surely the same might be said of Lord Pentland's death. May we all be so fortunate, and so courageous.

Forty Days

Yesterday marked forty days since my two friends died, in different cities at almost the same moment. After forty days, the thought of their disappearance is not as disturbing as it was in the beginning. I am more able to view this as a part of life. In a way I don't fully understand, I know they are still part of the greatness of life.

Thinking about my friends and about this greatness, I see all life on this earth as a cohesive, living, breathing organism with a specific quality and a specific place in the universe—the ladder of being. Within that organism we are all equally *particles*, united not only by our place in this ladder but by our purpose and our common relation to the Source.

Dear friends, I wish you well. You have served. You have loved. You are loved.

Never forget, life lives forever.

And now, why do I want to love the idea of death? It's become more personal. It's about facing my own mortality. It's also about feeling loss. Those loved friends and family members who have died are greatly missed. There are many moments when I wish to have only five minutes with a loved one. Like Aeneas, I would wish to embrace my father or my mother and find "...the form, reached for in vain, escaped/Like a breeze between his hands," as Heaney writes. If nothing else, I sometimes wish to hear their voices in a dream, and this has happened, but it's never quite enough. Always, there is a longing for the living person, the body and the spirit that fills that body. Thankfully, this longing is sometimes soothed in the inner silence by a whispered knowledge that tells me nothing or no one really dies. The disappearance of those dear people is just the beginning of an entirely new existence, for them and for me. How to live the final moment of life on earth that is, more than any other moment, a real and unique beginning?

Remembering Everything

Death is disappearance. It is loss, and it is also a huge mystery. Many years ago, one of my daughters asked me, "What happens when we die?"

She was just a little girl and this was a serious question. I could have made up an answer, but the moment was too important for a lie or even a half-truth. I tried to be honest. I pondered, and after a little pause, said, "We go back to where we were before we were born."

Because both girls were under the age of six, I hoped that they were close enough to their own beginnings to be satisfied with this answer. They seemed to be able to take it in and I hope something of that moment we shared then has stayed with them throughout the years.

I think about that answer often. More and more, it seems to be true. Trying to imagine where I was before I was born is not any more difficult than imagining where I will go when I die. Behind all this imagining lingers more big questions. Who am I? What am I? I remember discovering for myself that love is an energy. If that is true, and I believe it is, then I may be an energy, too. Or perhaps I am a complex of energies not always in relation with each other, but striving, wishing for harmony.

If it's true that when we die we return to where we came from when we were born—I believe it is—this implies that what I think of as myself, what makes me *me*, might be a kind of energy. At the very beginning of life in a human being—and in many other life forms—when two energies, male and female, find each other and unite, a third energy is called, and together, they make something new. This new energetic entity consists of three or more individual centers of energy, which inhabit a form that grows and develops. When the energetic entity leaves this form, all movement stops. The breath stops. It is the death of the body. That is almost as far as I can go from my own experience and knowledge. I know from my own experience that the energy of the body as well as the energy of the mind and the energy of the feeling are unique, with differing tempos and qualities and tastes. In life, they may or may not be in relation with each other. Most often, it takes hard work to support their unity, and I have to face the fact that my concept of unity may be quite wrong.

At death these energies may leave their container at their own tempo, depending on their previous relation to each other and their strength or weakness. I have had some experience of this but mostly this is speculation. It's more important, I believe, to trust the idea of *return*.

Perhaps the return to where I came from at birth means returning to the Source—to Nothingness or to Silence. Perhaps it's more complicated. The qualities that comprise an individual person, which are born with that person—each person is surely a more or less unique energetic entity—may originate in different places and return at death to those places. Perhaps memories of other realms or other lifetimes, individual quirks and talents inherited from parents, and qualities and capacities developed intentionally, such as a mind strong enough to remain present through challenging circumstances, color our essential energies or create new energies of a finer nature, preparing them to return again to where they came from—perhaps again to life on earth. Much of what is said about life after death, or before birth, is probably educated guesswork or information enforced by tradition. But there may be hints within one's own experience. There are certain true things, such as change, impermanence, the inexorable, essential process of transformation, ultimate joy, living silence, and more, which can be which can be contemplated, for understanding. They are all worth remembering.

At this stage of my life my wish to learn to love the idea of death is even deeper than it was when I began my experiments in learning. I am not as interested in learning more about the facts of death, although that will be inevitable. Grief, sadness, the pain of separation and disappearance are facts that must be experienced and lived through—there is no way to avoid them. But what, if anything, does the *idea* of death mean?

This question has tantalized me for many years. I have come closer to understanding it, and then, in forgetting, farther away. Now, I wish to understand the meaning of death, and through understanding, feel the energy of love, if only momentarily.

I try to look more and more directly at several *facts*. Over the last few years several friends have died. A few months ago one of my sisters died; she has disappeared from this world. My husband is increasingly frail as he nears the century mark. I know that some of my loved ones could disappear at any time—and my own death could happen at any moment. I know these facts are true, but the *feeling* is missing. How can I revive the feeling of past experiences of death recorded in my journals and notes or in my memory? Can these facts enter another world, the realm of feeling, where understanding is born? Then death would become an *idea*, an idea that would shine light on the largest questions: Who am I? Why was I born? What will happen when I die?

I think often of Sri Ramana Maharashi's experience of his own death and the Illumination that accompanied it. He was 16. Suddenly, he had a strong fear of death. But it didn't shake him. He simply lay down, closed his eyes, and held his breath, questioning what it meant to die. In a process that sounds like reasoning, but that happened in a flash, he realized that even if his body died, he did not. He felt the voice of "I" within himself. He saw that the body dies, "but the Spirit that transcends it cannot be touched by death." The result of this experience supported him throughout the rest of his life. As a pupil described this event, "The boy became a sage and a saint."

I remember the joy I felt when Lord Pentland died and the dream that came to me a few months later in which he affirmed that feeling of joy. "We're alive," he told me in the dream, and the pure, shining happiness in his face and voice revealed the truth of it. I remember my mother's courage and intention, and her final moments, with awe and love. I remember my father as he was during our last conversation, his face relaxed and filled with wonder, completely different from a time several years earlier when, after a long session with specialist doctors, he said that it was all over, and "After you die there is nothing." And, I remember my beautiful sister whose intelligence, courage, and concern for others became more and more evident throughout an illness that slowly took away her ability to control her body but not her mind.

Appalled just now by my lack of feeling as I remember these loved ones, I try to be more aware of my body as I write. I try to feel what I'm feeling and know what I know, even if it's very little. Then, I begin to understand the importance of Gurdjieff's words, *"Remember yourself always and everywhere."*

The practice of self-remembering, accompanied by self-observation, changes one's life; I've seen it happen. Now I realize that this practice is also a preparation for a final remembering—remembering who I am and where I came from, remembering the energy and power received from the special moments and the special people in my life and the feeling and sensation of this body breathing, in life and in love, remembering everything all at once. And then—letting go of all of it.

I have arrived at the *idea of death*. Like any great idea, once you've come to it, you know it can never be defined, spelled out or written down. It must be lived.

Myself

When I told a friend about the book I was writing and mentioned a few chapter titles, he asked if there was a chapter on learning to love myself. I made a joke and reminded us both of the huge amount of material—books, articles, classes, and so on—about that very subject. How to love yourself! Too much for me, I said. No more material is needed. It's all out there. However, I added, even with so many books and classes available, I seldom meet anyone who has real self-love accompanied by unshakeable self-regard and self-respect. At any rate, I was satisfied with not having such a chapter in my book.

But, my friend's question about learning to love myself lingered. Today, this question came up again while I was sitting very still and very quietly in my favorite place in the Colorado morning sun. As I sat, a new thought came to me—this whole book is about loving myself. For example, how could I love my parents without loving what they created? How could I love my children and my pupils without loving what I wish for them? How could I love music without loving who I am when I listen to music and feel one with the performers and the composer? Everything I studied asked for my love and therefore, asked me to love myself.

Every aspect of the learning process became important, each step of the way—attending in the most simple direct way to what is hidden or lost and giving my attention again and again to all of this until the lost world was *experienced*. Then, taught by the experience itself, learning about love and how to do it.

In this way, there were more and more moments of being able to love, and of loving the Source as well as every bit and particle of what is being created and destroyed in every moment.

None of this could have happened without a very important realization. I realized that loving what is perceived as other is not possible without beginning and then continuing—without words or descriptions or concepts—to be who I am, and by being who I am, to feel love for myself. Loving myself is simply a by-product. It is the wondrous result of loving others.

Life

It's not that I don't love life—I just forget about it. Too busy, too distracted, too tired. The forgetting has many allies in this world and all seem to take me away from the facts of existence: the fact that I exist and the fact that what I perceive exists. Some traditions say it's all illusion, which may be true. But when the whole feeling of myself is present, and the whole sensation of my body is here, and when I stand in nature and know that it is alive and I am alive, I will not be distracted by such a thought that thinks it knows something called *illusion*. At such a moment, I can love life.

I need a new ability to receive such moments; that has become clear to me after years of trying to understand who I am and how I operate. There is a need to give up my fascination with so many distracting thoughts in order to receive a direct, real moment of being present and of seeing the truth. To learn to love life, I need to go deeper than thought. Material from the past—even material from my teachers or from the great scholars and traditions—too often returns as mere thought and becomes a distraction.

In facing these distractions, which seem to appear from all sides, can I recognize, and acknowledge, the facts? How to discriminate? How can all my parts—not only my mind, but also my feelings and my body—understand the fact that I am *alive* and that this other person, who may be a stranger, a friend or a companion, a parent or a child, is *alive?* And the sky, the stars, the air, the plants, the rocks, the wood—all of it is *alive*. Everything I see and hear, taste and touch and feel—it's all alive. It's all real.

It's been a good, long study, trying to learn how to love. And now, there are more moments of remembering that *everything* is alive. I simply know this is true, and this knowledge awakens my feelings and helps me come to my own aliveness.

At the same time, since beginning the study of what it means to love and how it's done, life has become even more challenging. Still, there are moments when being too busy, too distracted, or too tired is not enough. In those moments it's important to remember what it is to be able to love. And sometimes it's possible. The experiences gathered while learning how to love have given me something reliable. I remember what it is to be interested and to learn, to be more relaxed down deep in my body. And most important of all, I remember to love.

Through my own experience, I have learned many things about my life here on earth. There have been many events and experiences that began at my birth and will end at my death. These events have molded me and formed the person I am now. But, life is the animating energy within the form. When not too distracted, I am aware of the feeling of being alive, which this energy creates in my body, and aware that this feeling informs my mind and body—and gives me the ability to love. Life and love must surely exist in a relationship of mutual benefit. It doesn't matter where in the scale of existence I look. High or low, inside or out, I've never seen a manifestation of love that is not animated by the finest energy of life. I've never seen any particle of life in all its wondrous aspects without knowing it contains at least one drop of love's energy.

Supported by a special dream that showed me love is an energy, I began to understand its purpose, the reason for its existence—the energy of love creates relationship on all levels, it heals both the lover and the loved, it lifts us upward. How to recognize this energy? When it's present, I feel alive, and this almost always feels like a gift.

Yet love seldom exists in human beings clearly and consistently. Surely, I reasoned, human beings, of which I am one, are meant for this energy. But first we must know how dependent on circumstances it is, and wish for it to be volitional—to be able to love. I realized that this knowledge and this wish can be developed by studying one's life and actions, one's thoughts and feelings. This study, while attempting to love and live intentionally, provides the fuel.

Finding my way over the past few years has led me to a simple statement. To learn how to live as I wish to live—with intelligence, with honor, and with joy, while feeling kinship with other forms of life—requires learning how to love.

There is so much more to learn, but I am ready.

Acknowledgments

I would like to acknowledge all the help I have received in this lifetime. As the years pass, my life feels more and more blessed. I have known remarkable men and women who devoted their lives to the Gurdjieff Work—many of them studied with Gurdjieff himself. They tirelessly shared their knowledge and presence with me and with many others.

As well, on various occasions, I have received blessings from some very holy people, including the 16th Karmapa and H.H. Dalai Lama, the Orthodox Patriarch of Antioch and Swami Muktananda, as well as others not so well known. My family has been devoted to spiritual exploration and the wish to help others. My many friends have been without exception intelligent and talented, all striving to be real human beings.

That is one side of my life, the light side. The other side is darker. I have been plagued by times of depressions and anxieties, lacking confidence in myself or my talents, by broken relationships and lost opportunities. Despair has crept in, telling me that the once-experienced consciousness will never come again. Close family ties have been threatened by a life filled with too many demands. And now, sadly, I begin to outlive too many friends and companions on the way.

For all its richness and variety of people and places, it has been a life like many other lives—filled with blessings and with light, which gives us hope, and with darkness, which tests and asks us to wake up.

This is the place for acknowledgement, yet it is almost impossible to truly thank people for the sometimes hidden yet always strong support they have given. I feel that support sometimes like the deep foundation that protects a building from too much earthquake damage. The support of my family has been and continues to be my deepest protection. My father gave me his love, his passion for learning, and a wry sense of humor; my mother gave the gift of her care and beauty, behind which lived her pondering of the imponderable, and a secret wish for being. My daughters and sisters have always given me their love and respect. They have generously shared their wisdom with me, as well as with many, many others—and they know how to listen. All these women, along with three granddaughters, a niece, two great-granddaughters, and now, a new great-grandson—all of them are amazingly beautiful and, young or old, amazingly wise! From the youngest to the oldest, they inspire me; they meet the challenges and joys of their lives with honesty, grace, and perseverance.

My mostly female family has been fortunate in the men who have joined us, who support and love us. I am grateful for them, and also grateful for the warm acceptance and love of my husband's extended family, and of course, for him. To put it very simply, without him not much would be possible.

If it is almost impossible to truly thank the people in my life, it is even more impossible to express my gratitude for this life. I can only become silent, trying right now to feel the greatness of life itself, receiving what comes from the very source of life, allowing it to quiet my mind, enliven my body, and fill my heart as it shows me how to love.

www.ingramcontent.com/pod-product-compliance
Lightning Source LLC
Chambersburg PA
CBHW030941090426
42737CB00007B/499